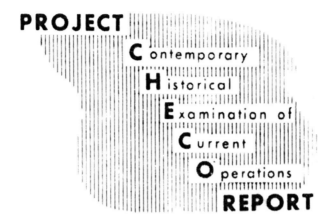

PROJECT
Contemporary
Historical
Examination of
Current
Operations
REPORT

FIXED WING GUNSHIPS IN SEA (JUL 69 - JUL 71)

30 NOVEMBER 1971

HQ PACAF

Directorate of Operations Analysis
CHECO/CORONA HARVEST DIVISION

Prepared by:

CAPT JAMES L. COLE, Jr.

Project CHECO 7th AF, DOAC

PROJECT CHECO REPORTS

The counterinsurgency and unconventional warfare environment of Southeast Asia has resulted in the employment of USAF airpower to meet a multitude of requirements. The varied applications of airpower have involved the full spectrum of USAF aerospace vehicles, support equipment, and manpower. As a result, there has been an accumulation of operational data and experiences that, as a priority, must be collected, documented, and analyzed as to current and future impact upon USAF policies, concepts, and doctrine.

Fortunately, the value of collecting and documenting our SEA experiences was recognized at an early date. In 1962, Hq USAF directed CINCPACAF to establish an activity that would be primarily responsive to Air Staff requirements and direction, and would provide timely and analytical studies of USAF combat operations in SEA.

Project CHECO, an acronym for Contemporary Historical Examination of Current Operations, was established to meet this Air Staff requirement. Managed by Hq PACAF, with elements at Hq 7AF and 7AF/13AF, Project CHECO provides a scholarly, "on-going" historical examination, documentation, and reporting on USAF policies, concepts, and doctrine in PACOM. This CHECO report is part of the overall documentation and examination which is being accomplished. It is an authentic source for an assessment of the effectiveness of USAF airpower in PACOM when used in proper context. The reader must view the study in relation to the events and circumstances at the time of its preparation--recognizing that it was prepared on a contemporary basis which restricted perspective and that the author's research was limited to records available within his local headquarters area.

ERNEST C. HARDIN, JR., Major General, USAF
Chief of Staff

ii

REPLY TO
ATTN OF: DOAD   30 NOV 1971

Project CHECO Report, "Fixed Wing Gunships in SEA, July 1969 -
July 1971" (U)

TO: SEE DISTRIBUTION PAGE

1. Attached is a SECRET NOFORN document. It shall be transported,
stored, safeguarded, and accounted for in accordance with applicable
security directives. SPECIAL HANDLING REQUIRED, NOT RELEASABLE TO
FOREIGN NATIONALS. The information contained in this document will
not be disclosed to foreign nations or their representatives.
Retain or destroy in accordance with AFR 205-1. Do not return.

2. This letter does not contain classified information and may be
declassified if attachment is removed from it.

FOR THE COMMANDER IN CHIEF

MIKE DELEON, Colonel, USAF   1 Atch
Chief, CHECO/CORONA HARVEST Division   Project CHECO Rprt (S/NF),
Directorate of Operations Analysis   30 Nov 71
DCS/Operations

iii

DISTRIBUTION LIST

1. SECRETARY OF THE AIR FORCE

   a. SAFAA 1
   b. SAFLL 1
   c. SAFOI 2
   d. SAFUS 1

2. HEADQUARTERS USAF

   a. AFNB. 1

   b. AFCCS
      (1) AFCCSSA 1
      (2) AFCVC 1
      (3) AFCAV 1
      (4) AFCHO 1

   c. AFCSA
      (1) AF/SAG. 1
      (2) AF/SAMI 1

   d. AF/SAJ. 1

   e. AFIGO
      (1) OSIIAP. 3
      (2) IGS 1

   f. AFSG. 1

   g. AFINATC 5

   h. AFACMI. 1

   i. AFODC
      (1) AFPRC 1
      (2) AFPRE 1
      (3) AFPRM 1

   j. AFPDC
      (1) AFDPW. 1

   k. AFRD
      (1) AFRDP. 1
      (2) AFRDQ. 1
      (3) AFRDQPC. 1
      (4) AFRDR. 1
      (5) AFRDQL 1

   l. AFSDC
      (1) AFSLP. 1
      (2) AFSME. 1
      (3) AFSMS. 1
      (4) AFSSS. 1
      (5) AFSTP. 1

   m. AFTAC. 1

   n. AFXO 1
      (1) AFXOB. 1
      (2) AFXOD. 1
      (3) AFXODC 1
      (4) AFXODD 1
      (5) AFXODL 1
      (6) AFXOOG 1
      (7) AFXOSL 1
      (8) AFXOOSN. 1
      (9) AFXOOSO. 1
     (10) AFXOOSS. 1
     (11) AFXOOSV. 1
     (12) AFXOOTR. 1
     (13) AFXOOTW. 1
     (14) AFXOOTZ. 1
     (15) AF/XOX 6
     (16) AFXOXXG. 1

3. MAJOR COMMAND

a. TAC

    (1) HEADQUARTERS
        (a) DO. 1
        (b) XP. 1
        (c) DOCC. 1
        (d) DREA. 1
        (e) IN. 1

    (2) AIR FORCES
        (a) 12AF
            1. DOO. 1
            2. IN 1
        (b) 19AF(IN). 1
        (c) USAFSOF(DO) . . . 1

    (3) WINGS
        (a) 1SOW(DOI) 1
        (b) 23TFW(DOI). . . . 1
        (c) 27TRW(DOI). . . . 1
        (d) 33TFW(DOI). . . . 1
        (e) 64TAW(DOI). . . . 1
        (f) 67TRW(DOI). . . . 1
        (g) 75TRW(DOI). . . . 1
        (h) 316TAW(DOX) . . . 1
        (i) 363TRW(DOI) . . . 1
        (j) 464TFW(DOI) . . . 1
        (k) 474TFW(DOI) . . . 1
        (l) 35TFW(DOI). . . . 1
        (m) 516TAW(DOX) . . . 1
        (n) 4403TFW(DOI). . . 1
        (o) 58TAC FTR TNG WG. . 1
        (p) 354TFW(DOI) . . . 1
        (q) 60MAWG(DOOXI) . . . 1

    (4) TAC CENTERS, SCHOOLS
        (a) USAFTAWC(DRA) . . . 1
        (b) USAFTFWC(DRA) . . . 1
        (c) USAFAGOS(EDA) . . . 1

b. SAC

    (1) HEADQUARTERS
        (a) DOX 1
        (b) XPX 1
        (c) DM. 1
        (d) IN. 1
        (e) NR. 1
        (f) HO. 1

    (2) AIR FORCES
        (a) 2AF(INCS) 1
        (b) 8AF(DOA). 2
        (c) 15AF(INCE). 1

c. MAC

    (1) HEADQUARTERS
        (a) DOI 1
        (b) DOO 1
        (c) CSEH. 1
        (d) MACOA 1

    (2) MAC SERVICES
        (a) AWS(HO) 1
        (b) ARRS(XP). 1
        (c) ACGS(CGO) 1

d. ADC

    (1) HEADQUARTERS
        (a) DO. 1
        (b) DOT 1
        (c) XPC 1

    (2) AIR DIVISIONS
        (a) 25AD(DOI) 1
        (b) 23AD(DOI) 1
        (c) 20AD(DOI) 1

e. ATC
    (1) DOSPI 1

RESEARCH NOTE

Most of the unpublished source materials for this report have been placed on microfilm. The message from 7th Air Force to the 8TFW dated 201130Z Apr 70, is on CHECO microfilm reel S-337 as is the letter from General Momyer to General Meyer dated 210009Z Jan 70. The letter from 7/13AF to 7th AF dated 270815Z Feb 70 which cites the performance of RLAF AC-47 crews is on CHECO microfilm reel S-364. Other documents are in the process of being microfilmed.

TABLE OF CONTENTS

FIGURES   <u>Follows Page</u>

FOREWORD

The unique demands of the operational environment in Southeast Asia dictated that the United States Air Force meet many mission requirements for which hardware did not exist. The lateral firing gunship evolved from this environment, and it constituted an immediate and effective solution for several tactical problems. This weapon system performed significantly in Southeast Asia. AC-47 gunship activity during 1965 and early 1966 was documented in four previous CHECO reports.[1] Another CHECO report, Night Close Air Support in RVN, also dealt in detail with AC-47 combat operations.[2] The Role of Gunships in SEA, a CHECO report dated 30 August 1969, recounts the continuing mission of the AC-47 as well as the introduction and employment of AC-119G, AC-119K, and AC-130A gunships in 1968 and 1969.[3]

The effectiveness of this unique weapon system generated significant interest at all command levels, and the combat role of gunships merits further attention and analysis. This report updates previous gunship studies with special emphasis on new developments in the AC-130 weapon system. This report also examines the current performance and effectiveness of the AC-47, long noted for its role in providing close air support for troops in contact; the AC-119G/K which functioned in armed reconnaissance and close air support roles; and the AC-130 which covered the whole spectrum of gunship operations but performed primarily as a night interdiction weapon system.

OVERVIEW

Side firing gunships were effective in combat. Their extended
loiter capability and relatively slow speed, coupled with devastating
firepower and sophisticated sensors, enabled them to accurately strike
targets and perform missions which were beyond the capabilities of most
other attack and fighter aircraft.

These weapon systems performed a variety of missions effectively.
The AC-47 "Spooky" gunship provided accurate close air support for outposts, hamlets, and friendly field units under night attack, as well as
airborne alert for airbase defense, air cover for night medevac operations, convoy escort, airborne command and control of jet fighter strikes
and harassment and interdiction of enemy base areas and lines of communication. The AC-47 proved the effectiveness of lateral firing weapon
systems in the USAF and paved the way for the development of more
sophisticated and effective gunships.

The fact that the AC-47 did not fade into obscurity with the advent
of more advanced gunships is significant. The ruggedness and reliability
of the AC-47, along with its capability for operating from relatively
unimproved airfields, made it an ideal weapon system for unconventional
warfare. Its simplicity and commonality to so many nations of the world
also made it an ideal gunship for nations with limited technical and
financial resources. It was well-suited for the South Vietnamese Air
Force and the Royal Laotian Air Force.

The AC-119G "Shadow" was suitable for providing close air support. In operations over Cambodia, it was equally useful for troops in contact (TIC) missions, convoy escort, armed reconnaissance, and enemy harassment.

The AC-119K "Stinger" gunship was able to perform all of the missions of the earlier gunship models. The 20mm cannon carried by the AC-119K increased its effectiveness against trucks.

The AC-130A "Spectre" gunships, equipped with bigger guns and sophisticated sensors, received high marks in all phases of operations. Its proficiency as a truck killer, however, overshadowed its potential for other tasks. It was exceptionally effective in a close air support role, and could deliver supporting fire through an obstructing cloud deck, despite some equipment difficulties. As with other gunships, the AC-130 was relatively vulnerable and incapable of contending with surface-to-air missiles or heavy concentrations of antiaircraft artillery. Technological innovations continued to make important contributions to the capabilities and combat effectiveness of the AC-130 and the future portended even greater advancements in the sophistication and effectiveness of gunships. But there were limitations on what gunships could be expected to do and where they could operate.

CHAPTER I

AC-47 COMBAT OPERATIONS

Early Employment

Initially there was some skepticism regarding the validity of arming an "ancient" cargo aircraft and using it for strike missions,[4/] but the war in Vietnam confronted the United States Air Force with a host of thorny problems which demanded immediate solutions. On 15 December 1964, the FC-47 was first employed in combat. This first mission and subsequent missions were quite successful, and Headquarters, Pacific Air Forces (PACAF) decided that this weapon system should be employed in greater numbers. Employment of armed C-47s would release some fighter aircraft from their commitment to night operations, and the presence of armed C-47s with night illumination flare capability would release C-123s from outpost defense duties and facilitate their employment in an airlift capacity.[5/]

The designation of the aircraft was changed from FC-47 to AC-47 and the 4th Air Commando Squadron, with a complement of 20 aircraft, was deployed to the Republic of Vietnam on 14 November 1965. The mission of the 4th Air Commando Squadron was confined primarily to night operations, and according to Seventh Air Force Ops Order 411-65, the AC-47 was: "To respond with flares and firepower in support of hamlets under night attacks, supplement strike aircraft in the defense of friendly forces and provide long endurance escort for convoys."[6/]

The aircraft was extremely effective in its assigned roles, but it soon became apparent that it could perform a variety of other tasks as well. The AC-47 was well-suited for air base defense against rocket, mortar, and ground assaults. The extended loiter capability of the AC-47 enabled two aircraft flying consecutive combat air patrols to maintain an airborne alert over a base from sundown to sunrise. The presence of the AC-47s probably deterred many attacks, and the aircraft's quick response and devastating firepower were instrumental in breaking off many attacks when they did occur. [7/]

AC-47s also found useful employment in covering night medevac operations. Friendly field units often sustained serious casualties during night operations, which could not wait for a routine medical evacuation the next morning. An AC-47 would "prep" the area around the proposed landing zone with its 7.62mm miniguns and then guide the medevac helicopters to the area. The gunship stood by to suppress any ground fire directed at the helicopters and provided illumination if requested. After the pickup had been made, the AC-47 would aid the helicopter in safely clearing the landing zone and returning to base.

The AC-47 was particularly well-suited for extended defense of long range reconnaissance patrols, providing protective cover throughout the night with firepower and flare support as required until a helicopter evacuation could be effected in the morning. In some cases, an AC-47 would actually cover a team extraction during the hours of darkness.*

* AC-47s were equipped with UHF, VHF, HF, and FM radios.

AC-47 "SPOOKY" GUNSHIPS

FIGURE 1

AC-47 "Spooky" Gunship Making Firing Pass:
Note 12° Declined Guns - SUU III/A Gun Pod

FIGURE 2

The AC-47 also found useful employment in escorting convoys. The aircraft's extended loiter capability, relatively slow air speed and devastating firepower made it ideal for this mission. Often, the mere presence of a Spooky overhead was sufficient to guarantee the safe passage of a truck convoy or tank column, even during the hours of darkness.

The AC-47 also functioned as a harassment and interdiction weapon system. If their services were not needed elsewhere, Spooky aircrews would attack enemy infiltration routes and rest areas. These activities blunted the enemy's initiative and deprived him of privileged sanctuaries.

AC-47 crews were often called upon to control night air strikes by jet fighters. An AC-47 was often the first aircraft to arrive on the scene when an outpost, hamlet or friendly field unit was under attack, since its reaction time was minimal from an airborne alert status. If jet fighters and a FAC were scrambled for the target, the former almost invariably arrived before the latter, and it was up to the AC-47 to function as the Forward Air Controller. Despite poor cockpit visibility and relatively awkward maneuvering characteristics, the AC-47s did a creditable job performing this mission.[8]

AC-47s were also employed for day and night armed reconnaissance in Laos. These missions were flown from 17 December 1965 to 20 July 1966, and 243 enemy trucks were destroyed or damaged during that period.[9] Although these missions were relatively successful, four crews were lost to enemy fire. Since the interdiction force consisted of an average

3

of 10 aircraft and 13 crews, such losses were considered unacceptable. The prohibitive loss rate, coupled with the limitations of the AC-47s small caliber weapons, precipitated the decision to withdraw the aircraft from Laos in July 1966.

From a conceptual phase marked by skepticism and doubt, the AC-47 developed into what was termed "one of the most successful and practical weapons for point defense and night close air support operations in the Republic of Vietnam."[10] (See Figure 3 for a listing of AC-47 characteristics and components.)

Although intended for use against guerrillas, the aircraft was able to survive and perform effectively in a permissive environment after the conflict in Vietnam expanded in scope and intensity to the level of a conventional war. The installation of armored flare bins enhanced the aircraft's survivability. Nevertheless, the AC-47's chances for survival were not good in an area of concentrated automatic weapons and anti-aircraft artillery. The 1965-1966 air operations in Laos clearly demonstrated this fact. Since the aircraft was usually employed to provide close air support for troops in contact rather than destroying trucks, they generally avoided dense concentrations of antiaircraft fire.

The AC-47 had several attributes which enhanced its usefulness. It was durable, reliable, and relatively inexpensive to operate. These factors made it popular with newly emerging nations, and due to its worldwide ubiquity, pilots of these nations often had C-47 experience.

4

SPOOKY COMPONENTS AND CHARACTERISTICS

GUNSHIP	SPOOKY
ACFT	AC-47
MISSION	AREA DEFENSE
AREA/TARGET	IN-COUNTRY AND OUT-COUNTRY/TROOPS IN CONTACT
ARMAMENT	3 x 7.62mm MINIGUNS FAST: 6,000 RDS/MIN (MXU-470/A) SLOW: 3,000 RDS/MIN
ARMOR	
ORDNANCE	21,000 RDS*
FCS	NONE-GUNSIGHT: FIXED RETICLE
TGT ACQ	VISUAL
ILLUMINATION	24-56 FLARES* MANUALLY DISPENSED
REACTION AIRSPEED	130K TAS
OPERATING ALTITUDE	3,000 FT AGL (OPTIMUM)
FUEL DURATION	7+00 HOURS
TURNAROUND	30 MINUTES
ESCORTS	NONE
AIRCREW	2 PILOTS 1 NAV 2 GUNNERS 1 LOADMASTER 1 FLT ENGINEER
ONE ENGINE OUT	UNSATISFACTORY AT COMBAT GROSS WEIGHT

* Varies According to Mission

FIGURE 3

The AC-47 itself was basically a simple weapon system with no sophisticated electronic sensors or other complicated equipment. Target acquisition and attack were primarily functions of acquiring the target visually and maneuvering the aircraft to the proper firing position, an easy maneuver for an experienced C-47 pilot. The AC-47 thus represented an ideal means with which to provide a small nation with a cheap, efficient and effective strike capability, particularly for close air support. [11]

The Vietnamese Air Force (VNAF)

The advent of the more sophisticated AC-119G/K and AC-130A gunships and the initiation of the VNAF Improvement and Modernization Program resulted in the transfer of USAF AC-47s to the VNAF. On 31 August 1969, the 817th Combat Squadron (CS) VNAF, was rated combat ready (C-1) as a gunship squadron. This was accomplished one month before the planned date. The 817th CS with 16 AC-47s at Tan Son Nhut Airfield represented the VNAF's sole gunship capability throughout 1970 and the first half of 1971. A second squadron, the 819th (AC-119G) was scheduled to be activated by 1 September 1971. [12]

The combat operations of the 817th CS were extremely successful. The squadron consistently fulfilled its operational commitments which involved eight aircraft per night in either an airborne or ground alert status. [13]

One advisor specifically stated that "they have never failed to meet a target commitment." [14] By December 1969, the Vietnamese AC-47 or "Fire Dragons" had replaced USAF AC-47s in Military Region (MR) 4. Soon they assumed responsibility for all four Military Regions covering the entire country from the Ben Hai River to the Ca Mau Peninsula. The 817th CS deployed alert aircraft to Da Nang, Pleiku, and Binh Thuy Air Bases (ABs) to fulfill mission requirements and provide responsive gunship support for all four MRs (Figures 4, 5, and 6 show VNAF gunship operational status). On target, tactical operations of the VNAF AC-47 aircrews appeared to be generally outstanding.[15/]

An excellent example of the skill and resourcefulness of VNAF AC-47 pilots is found in the performance of Captain Huynh Van Tong on 17 October 1969. On that night, while commanding an AC-47 on airborne alert over Binh Thuy Air Base, RVN, Captain Tong was directed to support a Vietnamese Army outpost at Phung Hiep which was under attack and in danger of being overrun.[16/] Captain Tong provided immediate firepower and flare support for the outpost. Additional air support was requested, and USAF F-100s were dispatched to aid in the defense of the outpost. In addition to his own on-target operations, Captain Tong functioned as a Forward Air Controller (FAC) directing the F-100s during their strikes and coordinating air operations over the target. Captain Tong and his crew flew three sorties in defense of the outpost returning to Binh Thuy to rearm after each expenditure of ammunition and flares. The VNAF AC-47 expended 63,000 rounds of 7.62mm ammunition and 150 illumination flares in support of the outpost, and the attack was repulsed with heavy enemy losses.[17/] This performance was exemplary

VNAF AIRCREWS (GUNSHIP AC-47)

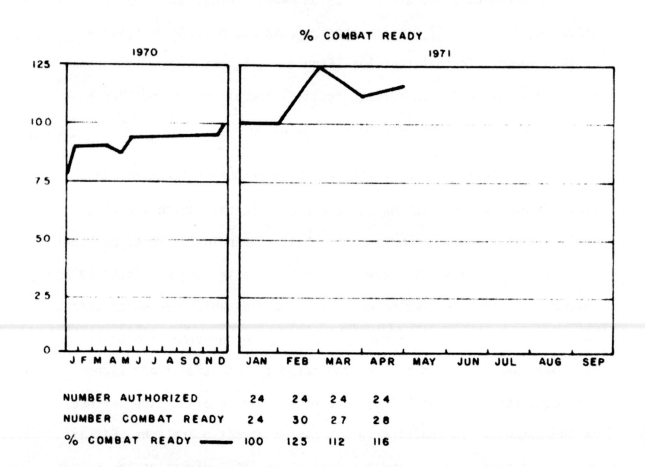

% COMBAT READY

	JAN	FEB	MAR	APR
NUMBER AUTHORIZED	24	24	24	24
NUMBER COMBAT READY	24	30	27	28
% COMBAT READY	100	125	112	116

SOURCE VNAF STATUS REVIEW APR 71

FIGURE 4

AIRCRAFT STATUS (AC-47)

% O/R, NORM & NORS

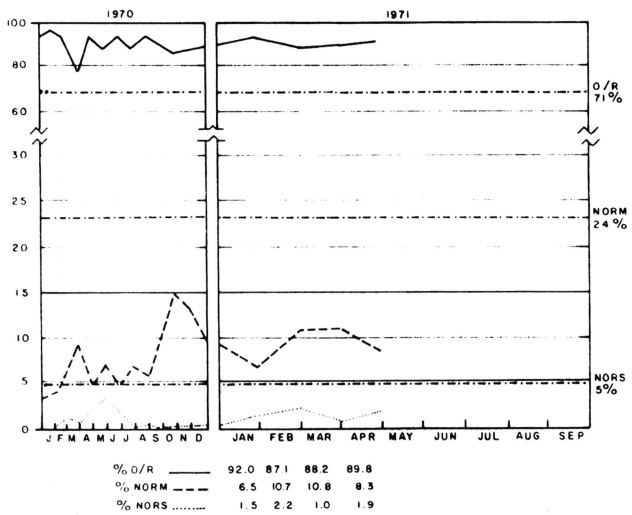

% O/R ————	92.0	87.1	88.2	89.8
% NORM ― ― ―	6.5	10.7	10.8	8.3
% NORS	1.5	2.2	1.0	1.9

SOURCE VNAF STATUS REVIEW

VNAF AIRCRAFT UTILIZATION (AC-47)

AVERAGE HOURS PER POSSESSED AIRCRAFT

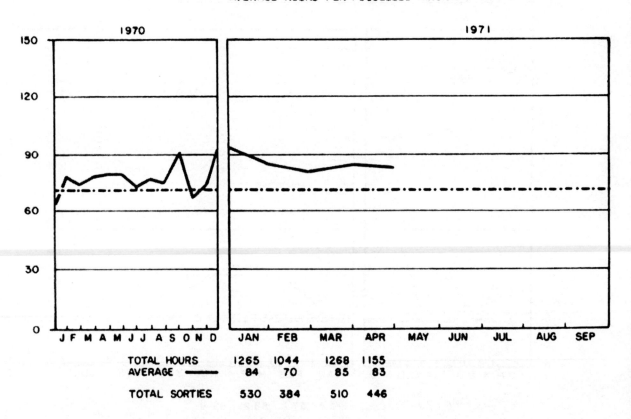

	JAN	FEB	MAR	APR
TOTAL HOURS	1265	1044	1268	1155
AVERAGE ———	84	70	85	83
TOTAL SORTIES	530	384	510	446

SOURCE: VNAF STATUS REVIEW APR 71

--- STANDARD: 75 HOURS / ACFT / MONTH

FIGURE 6

not only with respect to the skillful employment of the AC-47, but the expert control of the USAF aircraft as well. The USAF Advisory Team (AFAT-5) was especially impressed with Captain Tong's effort, and he was awarded the Air Medal for his outstanding display of professional skill and airmanship.[18/]

Another excellent example of the outstanding work of VNAF AC-47 crews occurred on 7 November 1969. On that night, Fire Dragon 03, commanded by Major Nguyen Sue Son, was on airborne alert over Tan Son Nhut Airfield when at 0310 hours, he was directed by the Tactical Air Control Center (TACC) to proceed to Phuoc Thon hamlet. A unit of the Army of the Republic of Vietnam (ARVN) was being overrun by an estimated battalion of Viet Cong (VC). Major Son established communications with the ARVN commander, who called for flares and fire support. Major Son laid a ring of minigun fire around the perimeter of the hamlet and then along a creek bed, which was suspected to be the path that the VC were using to approach the hamlet.

Foreseeing that he would use most of his ammunition and flares before all the VC could be driven off, the Major asked for more aircraft from the TACC, which then sent a USAF AC-47. Major Son learned, however, that the USAF Spooky gunship had no ARVN interpreter on board and that the ground troops had no American liaison or advisory people with them. With no FAC available in the area to guide the USAF Spooky, Major Son, who spoke good English, decided to assume the FAC role, and directed the Spooky in its flare drop and firing until, like Major Son's plane, the USAF AC-47 was out of ammunition and flares.

The Fire Dragon's commander then called for more help, and two UH-1 helicopter gunships were sent, which he also directed. Staying in the area, he acted as FAC for a USAF AC-119 which relieved the UH-1s. The attack was finally broken off by the VC, largely because of the VNAF AC-47 commander's resourcefulness and capacity in serving as liaison, FAC and interpreter for all air and ground elements, while he continued to pilot his aircraft. Major Son was awarded the Air Medal for his outstanding performance.

Such examples of VNAF pilots' understanding and prosecution of the air war were said to be far from rare. There was written testimony in the files of AFAT-1 attesting to the respect the 817th earned during its first six months of operations from FACs and ARVN units, U.S. Army outposts and mobile ground units, U.S. and Vietnamese Navy riverine forces, U.S. Army helicopter gunships crews and USAF tactical fighter crews.

There were several reasons for the success of the VNAF AC-47 program. Initially, the weapon system was well-tested and proven effective by USAF AC-47 squadrons. The skill and experience of VNAF AC-47 pilots did much to guarantee the success of the program. Some VNAF pilots had been flying C-47 aircraft for 10 or more years. The average pilot in the 817th CS had approximately 2,000 hours in the C-47. [19] Fortunately, the VNAF pilots were able to concentrate their efforts on learning to

aim and fire the guns rather than learning to fly the aircraft. The
Vietnamese aircrew members were also familiar with the local terrain;
this was a great help in performing the AC-47 mission. One USAF colonel
commented: "It takes our people a while to become familiar with the
terrain, the hamlets, the fields, and the forests--where one stops and
the other starts. The Vietnamese seem to be able to acquire the target
much faster at night."[20]

Good maintenance is essential to any successful flying operation
and VNAF operational readiness (OR) rates for their AC-47s were outstanding.[21] Experience provided the key, for many VNAF maintenance personnel
worked on C-47s before being assigned to the 817th CS. Some maintenance
problems developed with the MXU 470/A gun module, but they were gradually
resolved as the VNAF aerial gunners gained more experience with the
weapon.[22]

The 817th CS was affected by the accelerated pace of the VNAF
Improvement and Modernization (I&M) Program. Established squadrons
such as the 817th were used as a source of pilots to provide an
experience base for newly formed squadrons. The practice diluted the
experience level of the established squadrons and hampered their
operational effectiveness to some extent. It takes time to build
a significant experience base for a rapidly expanding Air Force. But
the VNAF had no workable alternative to drawing experienced personnel
from established squadrons.

9

Barrel Roll

Other significant AC-47 operations were being conducted concurrently with the VNAF development of a gunship capability. The United States Air Force was gradually transferring its AC-47 assets to the VNAF, but USAF aircrews were still employing the weapon system well into 1970. In March 1969, the 4th Special Operations Squadron (SOS) had sent a detachment TDY to Udorn Royal Thai Air Force Base (RTAFB), Thailand, for operations in the Barrel Roll (northern Laos). Headquarters PACAF and the Air Attache in Laos requested that the three AC-47 aircraft assigned TDY to Udorn RTAFB be located there permanently because "the gunships were critical in the defense of friendly Laotian outposts (Lima Sites), and the presence of gunships was necessary to offset the increased enemy activity in the Barrel Roll around the Lima Sites."[23/]

On 10 December 1969, the AC-47s were permanently assigned to the 432d Tactical Reconnaissance Wing, but operational control was exercised by Headquarters 7th Air Force (7AF) through Blue Chip (Command Post) and the Airborne Battlefield Command and Control Center (ABCCC). Requirements for tactical employment were originated by Headquarters Seventh/Thirteenth Air Force (7/13AF) from data supplied by Controlled American Source (CAS) and the Air Attache (AIRA) in Laos.

Although the AC-47s had effectively performed a variety of tasks in the Republic of Vietnam (RVN) and had previously flown interdiction missions in Laos, their primary mission in the Barrel Roll was support of troops in contact (TIC). Since they were not hunting trucks, the

AC-47s avoided heavy concentrations of enemy antiaircraft artillery (AAA). The aircraft were equipped with three 7.62mm miniguns, Mark 24 illumination flares and Mark 6 ground marker flares. AC-47s were scrambled to a target from either an airborne or ground alert status and when they arrived in the target area they normally operated under the direction of an English-speaking Forward Air Guide (FAG). The FAG would mark his position with a flare, strobe light, fire or even a flashlight, and the AC-47 would descend to 3,000 feet above ground level (AGL) to fire a marking burst with the 7.62mm miniguns. The FAG would adjust the fire and the AC-47 would respond accordingly.

Adverse weather, particularly during the rainy season, hampered AC-47 operations as did the similarity of terrain features in Laos. Low ceilings often prevented the gunships from descending to firing altitude. Rugged terrain often complicated and prolonged the process of initially locating the FAG, especially if he was not established in a visible fortified position. Nevertheless, the AC-47s were highly effective in their mission of providing close air support for friendly forces in Laos. The following figures represent the efforts of only three aircraft and even these statistics represent only a small measure of the AC-47s effectiveness: [24]/

	Sorties	Rounds of 7.62 Expended	Rounds of Mark 24 Expended	KBA
November 1969	40	739,900	647	RNO*
December 1969	68	1,156,900	1,167	92
January 1970	75	1,374,400	1,368	56
February 1970	88	1,355,200	1,342	462
March 1970	98	1,438,900	898	38
April 1970	86	1,420,150	972	8
May 1970	52	821,500	599	RNO*

*RNO: Results Not Observed

The Killed by Air (KBA) figures represent only those confirmed by body count. The actual tally was probably higher, for friendly forces normally did not reconnoiter the area until the following morning, thus giving the retreating enemy significant time to recover their dead. Numerous blood trails leading from the battle areas appeared to corroborate this assertion. On many occasions the friendly forces did not even sweep the battle area, since the probability of sustaining additional friendly casualties just to count enemy bodies hardly constituted a justifiable risk.

The figures presented cover the months of peak activity during the dry season (December through April). The pace slackened somewhat during the rainy season. Although the KBA for January, March, and April were low, the Air Attache in Vientiane reported that the gunships were frequently commended for their support of remote outposts under night attack. The knowledge that gunships were readily available stiffened the resistance of the defenders in the isolated outposts.[25/]

Although the USAF was rapidly depleting its AC-47 inventory in favor of AC-119G/K and AC-130A gunships, the unique requirements for close air support in northern Laos continued to exist. The three AC-47 gunships at Udorn RTAFB were transferred to the Royal Laotian Air Force (RLAF) under the Military Assistance Program (MAP). The last USAF AC-47 mission was flown on 29 May 1970 to facilitate the preparation of the aircraft for delivery to the RLAF on 1 June 1970.[26/] The following comment is indicative of the AC-47's performance:[27/]

> As the gunships' activities drew to a close, several favorable communications were received praising the operations of the last AC-47 gunships in the Air Force inventory.

Royal Laotian Air Force (RLAF)

The addition of "Spooky" gunships to the RLAF inventory marked the commencement of a new and interesting chapter in the history of the AC-47. USAF AC-47s effectively supported Royal Laotian Government (RLG) forces under night attack. A Mobile Training Team (MTT) was established at Udorn RTAFB, Thailand, and the first Laotian aircrew completed the AC-47 checkout on 1 August 1969. The following comments by the USAF AC-47 instructor indicated that the RLAF AC-47 program would require much additional time and effort if it were to be successful:[28/]

13

> *Captain Tousane flew one-half of the total effective mission time. Tactical Air Navigation (TACAN) new to him. Wants to talk in Lao. Can't read maps too well. Very good stick and rudder. Above average shot. Gunner throws up all the time.*

The RLAF AC-47s were indeed plagued by a multitude of operational and mechanical difficulties when they were first employed. Laotian pilots had limited instrument or night flying experience, and they were consequently fearful of flying at night in a combat zone and in the mountains with the additional danger of weather. Even when the aircraft were finally airborne over a target, they were plagued by maintenance difficulties. After receiving an AC-47 at Savannakhet, the Air Operations Center (AOC) Commander made the following comment:[29]

> *The AC-47 program has gone over like the proverbial lead balloon. To quote a conscientious crew member; "The aircraft will not fly, but if it could fly, I cannot talk to the troops because the radios do not work, and if the radios worked I cannot help them because the guns do not shoot." Despite the initial flops, local interest in the program remains high and the residents of Keng Kok are still a little puzzled and awed by the strange "DAKOTA" that shot "ROCKETS" all over their lake.*

As the Laotian crews became accustomed to their new equipment, maintenance difficulties were gradually resolved, but an increase in the number of RLAF gunships placed an additional strain on the program. The RLAF simply did not have enough pilots with the proper experience for AC-47 night combat operations. Consequently, the U.S. Ambassador made the following proposal:[30]

The original program for C-47 MTT training envisioned the production of sufficient aircrews and IPs to support a fleet of five AC-47 aircraft. Since that time the AC-47 fleet has been increased to eight in number. In addition, operational necessity has precluded the availability of the trained IPs for use in the instruction role and has required their use as operational pilots. With the manning required for the use of 24 C-47 aircraft and eight AC-47 aircraft, the lack of pilots qualified for night and instrument flight conditions will continue to be a problem. We envision the C-47 MTT as the method of alleviating this problem, rather than only producing qualified AC-47 crews. In short, all existing and future C-47 crews must receive night, instrument and some degree of tactical training. When this training is accomplished, the RLAF could then reasonably be expected to simultaneously support the tactical effort as well as a training program.

Aircrew experience remained a "continuing problem" with RLAF personnel, but the situation gradually improved.[31/] A sufficient level of expertise finally developed so that Laotians were instructing Laotians in the AC-47 with Americans supervising the whole program.

Training difficulties were being overcome, but operational problems still existed. Brass from expended ammunition was sold and the money thus obtained was divided among the aircrew members and base personnel.[32/] Consequently, the AC-47s always expended their ammunition on "fast rate," regardless of whether they had a target or not.[33/] The cost of replacing barrels, batteries, and guide bars for the guns in addition to replacing the expended ammunition was high. Time and effort on the part of the Americans helped to correct this problem, as is indicated by a USAF advisor to the RLAF:[34/]

15

> *One of the biggest improvements in saving material,*
> *especially the guns. Before, they had a policy--*
> *you have to get on targets, you have to expend,*
> *you have to leave--. We were really burning up the*
> *barrels, the batteries and the bolts and in six*
> *months they would go thru 700 gun barrels, 110 bat-*
> *teries and many guide bars. A guide bar is a simple*
> *piece of metal about the size of a stapler but costs*
> *about $184, and we were changing maybe 75 per month.*
> *So we tried to convince them to shoot slow rate--.*

The RLAF problems were manifold, and they proved to be a source of frustration and irritation to some of those attempting to develop a viable RLAF AC-47 capability. One official despairingly asserted: [35]/ "RLAF aircrews (AC-47) do not possess the professional maturity necessary to operate as an effective fighting force."

But according to the USAF advisor to the RLAF AC-47 program, the gunship's operational effectiveness and credibility improved significantly: [36]/

> *A year ago they had problems. The RLAF was strictly a*
> *VFR type of flying. Very few of them had instruments,*
> *never flew at night before, especially night weather.*
> *When they first started flying, they would fly about*
> *30 missions a month; their missions now are up to 211*
> *per month, and frankly it is quite surprising because*
> *we said they would never hit 200 per month. They are*
> *pushing 211 now and that was in February, the shortest*
> *month. Now they are flying an average sortie rate of*
> *eight per night out of Vientiane.*

The RLAF AC-47 program was still far from complete, but the effectiveness of the weapon system and the increasing experience and capability of the aircrews portended a self-sufficient and extremely effective RLAF close air support capability for troops in contact. Even then, the RLAF could boast that they "have never lost a site with a Spooky overhead."[37/]

Observations

The fact that the AC-47 did not pass into obscurity with the advent of larger and more sophisticated gunships is significant. The aircraft upheld the concept of lateral firing weapon systems and it represented a potent strike capability, particularly in unconventional warfare.

The C-47 was prevalent throughout the world, and it was a familiar aircraft to many pilots. It was a simple yet reliable aircraft and it was relatively easy to maintain. Consequently, the AC-47 weapon system was appropriate for employment by the VNAF and RLAF. The Thais and the Cambodians also developed an AC-47 capability. Although the USAF no longer employed the aircraft, the VNAF and RLAF were utilizing it for a wide variety of missions. Its primary function, however, remained that of providing close air support for troops in contact. The AC-47 established a record of combat excellence. This record would no doubt continue as long as the AC-47 was employed in the roles for which it was ideally suited, particularly night close air support in a permissive air environment.

CHAPTER II

AC-119G/K COMBAT OPERATIONS

Early Employment: AC-119G

The first AC-119G Shadow operational sortie was flown on 5 January 1969 and from that time until 8 March, the aircraft was in a combat evaluation phase. During this evaluation, primary emphasis was given to close air support for troops in contact, but the aircraft also flew armed reconnaissance and interdiction, as well as forward air controller missions. By 7 February 1969, the full complement of AC-119G aircraft had arrived in the Republic of Vietnam (RVN) and were initially located at Tan Son Nhut, Phan Rang, and Nha Trang Air Bases. [38/] The aircraft were assigned to the 17th Special Operations Squadron (SOS) of the 14th Special Operations Wing (SOW) and under the operational control of Hq 7AF. The aircraft performed all of its assigned missions in a satisfactory manner. The Shadow gunship operated much in the same manner as the AC-47, although the AC-119G Night Observation Device (NOD) and illuminator gave the aircraft an increased capability over the Spooky gunship. The aircraft functioned primarily as a close air support weapon system for troops in contact in RVN. (See Figure 7 for Shadow characteristics and components.)

AC-119Gs were deployed as needed to various bases including Phu Cat, Phan Rang, Da Nang, and Tan Son Nhut, but all Shadow aircraft were eventually stabilized and located solely at Phan Rang and Tan Son Nhut.

The flight at Phan Rang was tasked with the dual mission of providing close air support for troops in contact, primarily in Military Region II, and for training VNAF aircrews. The flight at Tan Son Nhut performed a threefold mission of providing close air support for troops in contact in Cambodia, escorting convoys and conducting armed reconnaissance in Cambodia. [39/]

Operations in Cambodia

The increased air and ground operations in Cambodia generated a requirement for 24-hour interdiction coverage of enemy supply routes. The AC-119G flight at Tan Son Nhut was tasked with this responsibility, and they were occasionally augmented by AC-119K Stinger gunships during periods of peak activity. Cambodia's relatively small geographical area enabled the AC-119G gunships to react quickly to enemy supply movements in almost any part of the country. Daytime operations posed no particular problems to the AC-119G crews. [40/] Constant surveillance by Forward Air Controllers (FACs) precluded the extensive establishment of anti-aircraft gun positions by the enemy, and the Shadow aircrews carefully avoided known high threat areas. Trucks and sampans were the primary targets of armed reconnaissance, and the AC-119G's 7.62mm ball ammunition proved fairly effective against both until the VC armored their sampans. In July 1970, AC-119Ks with their heavier firepower (20mm cannon) were called in to support this type operation. The AC-119Ks first used the 20mm HEI loads but found these ineffective against the armored sampans. The

19

SHADOW COMPONENTS AND CHARACTERISTICS

ACFT	AC-119G
MISSION	ARMED RECCE
AREA/TARGET	IN-COUNTRY/TROOPS IN CONTACT, OUT COUNTRY TROOPS IN CONTACT, CONVOY ESCORT
ARMAMENT	4 x 7.62mm MINIGUNS FAST: 6,000 RDS/MIN SLOW: 3,000 RDS/MIN
ARMOR	2,000 LBS
ORDNANCE	3.,500 RDS
FIRE CONTROL	COMPUTERIZED FCS INCORPORATING FULLY AUTO, SEMIAUTO, MANUAL FIRING, OFF-SET CAPABLE
TGT ACQ (SENSOR)	NIGHT OBSERVATION SIGHT (NOS)
ILLUMINATION	ILLUMINATOR 1.5 MILLION CANDLEPOWER WITH 20-40 DPG VARIABLE BEAM (20KW). 24 FLARES DISPENSED FROM LAUNCHER
REACTION AIRSPEED	180K TAS
OPERATING ALTITUDE	3,500 FT AGL (STANDARD)
FUEL DURATION	6+30
TURNAROUND	30 MIN
ESCORTS	NONE
AIRCREW	2 PILOTS 2 NAV: TABLE NAV, NOS OPR 1 ILLUM OPR 2 GUNNERS 1 FLT ENGINEER
ONE ENGINE OUT	UNSATISFACTORY AT COMBAT GROSS WEIGHT

FIGURE 7

AC-119G "SHADOW GUNSHIP: NOTE GUNPORTS FOR 7.62MM MINIGUNS

FIGURE 8

AC-119G "Shadow" Gunship in Firing
ATTITUDE: Note 7.62mm Miniguns

FIGURE 9

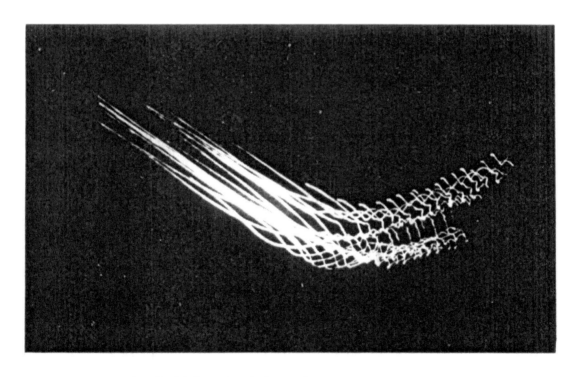

AC-119G "Shadow" Gunship Firing at Night

FIGURE 10

loads were changed to 20mm armor-piercing incendiaries (API) and the sampans were destroyed.

U.S. air support in Cambodia was centered around the AC-119G gunship. The AC-119Gs performed three types of missions. Troops in contact were first priority, followed by convoy escort and armed reconnaissance in turn.[41] On occasion, AC-119Gs performed all three missions on one sortie. The immediate result was the relief of the critical petroleum products shortage in Phnom Penh. Both river and road convoys were provided with escort.

Two or three days' advance notice was provided by the Navy planners for river convoys.[42] An AC-119G provided 24-hour coverage circling over the convoy at 3,500 feet. In addition, during daylight a FAC was in the area at 2,500 feet. Other air support during daylight consisted of an Army light fire team (one command and control helicopter, two Cobra helicopter gunships and two light observation helicopters) flying at or below 1,500 feet. These helicopters were stationed at Chi Lang and cycled between the convoy and Chi Lang for refueling. At night, the Navy provided two UH-1Bs and two OV-10s to accomplish the low altitude coverage. These Navy aircraft cycled between the convoy and the Navy command and control vessel anchored on the RVN side of the Mekong at Tan Chau. This composite of aircraft from the three services was designated an air cover package, and was controlled by 7AF.[43]

The escort of road convoys was difficult to plan, because the Cambodians scheduled their own road convoys and often gave no advance notice of intended movement. Escort of road convoys in most cases consisted of a single gunship or a FAC aircraft or both.<u>44/</u>

Armed reconnaissance was performed when there was no requirement to support TICs or escort convoys. While flying armed reconnaissance, the AC-119Gs were required to stay within 15 minutes flying time of the Phnom Penh-Kompong Cham region.<u>45/</u>

Shadow gunships were particularly effective in performing their convoy escort duties. The aircraft would fly in a large elliptical orbit directly overhead; often the Shadow aircrews worked in conjunction with a FAC who would actively search for enemy ambush preparations along the intended route of the convoy. If an ambush site was discovered or if an ambush was actually launched, the AC-119G immediately engaged the enemy with its 7.62mm miniguns. These tactics were equally effective in protecting river-borne traffic, as well as motorized convoys on highways and roads. The presence of the AC-119Gs was a major factor in keeping open the supply lines to Phnom Penh.

An excellent example of the AC-119Gs' ability to protect convoys is provided by a mission flown on 30 June 1971 in the area southwest of Phnom Penh. A 51 truck convoy was proceeding from Phnom Penh to Kompong Som along Route 4. A Forward Air Controller escorting the convoy observed intense enemy activity north of Route 4, and it appeared that the enemy was preparing to ambush the convoy. The FAC requested strike aircraft, and an AC-119G was diverted from a target northeast of Phnom Penh. The convoy had not yet reached the suspected ambush site, and the FAC decided to investigate further before clearing the Shadow to fire. The FAC's suspicions were confirmed and he cleared the AC-119G to attack the enemy forces. The AC-119G attacked the enemy troop concentrations and received heavy ground fire, including 12.7mm AW fire in return. [46/] The Shadow continued to engage the enemy until the last truck had safely passed the ambush site. [47/] When the AC-119G returned to base, it had flown 5.3 hours and expended 31,500 rounds of 7.62 ammunition. The extended loiter capability and devastating firepower of the Shadow gunship had done the job well. This was but one of numerous examples of the AC-119G's effectiveness.

AC-119Gs were also extremely effective in providing close air support for troops in contact. Body counts of enemy dead were difficult to obtain, for many of the attacks occurred during the hours of darkness. Friendly troops would not sweep the battle area until daybreak and this gave the enemy ample time to retrieve his dead. Many enemy attacks were broken off immediately when a Shadow appeared overhead.

Accomplishments during the last six months of 1970 and the first three months of 1971 vividly illustrate the combat effectiveness of the AC-119G/Ks in Cambodia. During that time period, the Shadow gunships supported by

22

Stinger gunships* were credited with 3,151 KBA (confirmed), 609 vehicles destroyed or damaged, 237 sampans destroyed and 494 sampans damaged.[48/] This remarkable record was achieved through perceptive and judicious employment of the AC-119s. The Cambodian air environment was relatively permissive, and there were no dense concentrations of enemy AAA. Identified high threat areas were carefully monitored and avoided by the Shadow gunships.

7.62mm Armor Piercing Incendiary Ammunition

A limited amount of 7.62mm armor piercing incendiary (API) ammunition was procured from the U.S. Army and used on a trial basis in the AC-119G. This ammunition was favorably received by the aircrews, because they believed it markedly enhanced the combat effectiveness of the Shadow gunships. The primary advantage of the API ammunition was that the pilots were able to precisely adjust their fire on each firing pass. Because the API rounds "sparkled" on impact, the pilot was able to see precisely where the bullets were impacting; such was not the case with standard ball and tracer ammunition. A secondary benefit was that the API was much more effective than ball ammunition against hard targets such as trucks and buildings. The following comments by AC-119G aircraft commanders constitute a representative cross section from mission reports during the test period in October 1970:[49/]

* During the last six months of 1970, the 18th SOS operated five AC-119K aircraft at its 17th SOS FOL (Tan Son Nhut AB) to provide the heavier firepower of the K series gunships.

*Is excellent for noting impact area as opposed to
regular 7.62mm. Should be a standard load.*

*Very good to see bullet impact point--also very
good to ignite dry or inflammable material--
recommend we use as standard load with tracer
mix.*

*FAC reported one motorcycle was knocked apart
on the road and others damaged. He also reported
that the API knocked the entire front wall out of
a house. Excellent, get more.*

If such operations were to continue, a development program was required to produce new 7.62mm API ammunition. Additional ammunition was not secured because of the cost of producing new 7.62mm API, but this ammunition was markedly superior to ball ammunition in certain respects. While the test program was being conducted, the use of 7.62mm ball and tracer ammunition most definitely enhanced the combat effectiveness of the AC-119G.

VNAF Improvement and Modernization

Following the activation of the VNAF 817th Combat Squadron (AC-47), a plan was developed for expanding Vietnamese gunship capability. AC-119Gs were being programmed for the VNAF and Vietnamese personnel and aircraft were slated to assume the mission of the 17th Special Operations Squadron (USAF AC-119Gs). The aircraft and facilities of the 17th SOS were to be turned over to the VNAF, and on 1 September 1971, the VNAF 819th Combat Squadron (AC-119G) was scheduled to be activated. 50/

A VNAF training schedule was developed to insure that the personnel in the squadron would indeed be ready for activation on the programmed date.[51/]   Phase I training was accomplished at Clinton County AFB, Ohio, where VNAF pilots received their C-119 checkout. Phase II training was accomplished by the 17th SOS at Phan Rang AB, RVN; this included a gunnery checkout, as well as additional ground and flight training. Phase III training and certification of VNAF aircrews was accomplished by the 17th SOS at Tan Son Nhut Airfield, RVN. By 14 April 1971, three VNAF AC-119G crews had completed all three phases of training and were certified combat ready. By 17 June 1971, an additional seven crews had completed their training and two more groups of seven crews each were slated to be complete by 1 August and 10 September respectively.[52/]

This training was accomplished smoothly and effectively by the 17th SOS concurrent with its performance of the AC-119G combat mission. Certain problem areas were identified during the course of VNAF training and the USAF instructors made a concerted effort to alleviate these problems before the 819th CS's scheduled activation date. Most of the VNAF aircraft commanders already had experience in C-119 transports. They were thus basically familiar with the aircraft and could concentrate their efforts on gunnery and on-target operations. Average total time for the VNAF aircraft commanders was about 4,000 hours, with anywhere from 500 to 1,000 hours of that total in C-119s.[53/] VNAF copilots, however, were relatively inexperienced; most were second lieutenants with an average total time of about 300 hours with 50 of that total in C-119s.[54/]

Most of the Vietnamese pilots were weak on instrument procedures and somewhat apprehensive about weather and night flying.[55/] It was

25

imperative to increase their proficiency and build their confidence as quickly as possible, for night operations were essential to effective gunship operations. This was accomplished by initially flying day gunnery missions with the VNAF crews to thoroughly acclimate them to AC-119G on-target operations; they were phased into the night operations. This technique worked quite well, for after being exposed to weather and associated instrument conditions during the daylight hours, they were much less apprehensive about night operations.[56/]

Crew coordination was also a significant problem for VNAF AC-119G aircrews. A smoothly functioning and well-coordinated crew was essential for effective gunship operations, particularly in the areas of target identification and on-target operations. The VNAF aircraft commanders had a tendency to try and do everything themselves and not listen to the other crew members. There were two reasons for this conflict. First, the experience level of the aircraft commander was usually far above that of his copilot, navigator, and NOD operator. A typical VNAF crew had a captain aircraft commander with about 4,000 hours total flying time and second lieutenants for the copilot, navigator, and NOD positions. Copilots and navigators were often hesitant to assert themselves in the face of the pilot's experience. A second aspect of the problem was found in the centralization of authority in a VNAF aircrew. In the words of one U.S. advisor, the VNAF believe that "the pilot is the boss."[57/] Navigators were hesitant to forcefully assert themselves in questions of target identification. Time, effort, and experience would result in a better comprehension of the complexity of the gunship mission and the necessity for crew coordination, so this problem was expected gradually to resolve itself.

The experience of the crew members varied greatly. Some had their first airplane ride when they flew to Phan Rang AB for training. The experience level of the first three VNAF AC-119G crews which included no aerial gunners, is shown below:[58]

Pilots	Total Flying Time (Operational)
Major	11,219
Captain	5,389
Captain	5,248

Copilots	
Second Lieutenant	314
Second Lieutenant	314
Second Lieutenant	300

Navigators	
First Lieutenant	2,600
Second Lieutenant	0
Second Lieutenant	0
Second Lieutenant	0
Second Lieutenant	0
Second Lieutenant	0

Flight Engineers	
Technical Sergeant	2,241
Technical Sergeant	125
Technical Sergeant	125

Illuminator Operators	
Technical Sergeant	2,134
Airman Basic	0
Airman Basic	0

These figures are only representative, but they indicate the source of some of the problems of crew coordination.

Crew experience and crew coordination remained key problems. Most of the aerial gunners, however, were drawn directly from the VNAF AC-47 squadron. These men had few problems, since they were already proficient with the MXU-470/A gun module, an item common to both the AC-47 and the AC-119G.

The I&M program for the activation of the 819th CS (VNAF) progressed according to schedule and the proficiency of the VNAF aircrews increased rapidly. On 15 August 1971, the VNAF aircrews were scheduled to take over AC-119G flight operations and on 1 September, the 819th CS was scheduled for activation. Progress had been good, and when one American advisor was questioned regarding the VNAF aircrews' ability to perform the AC-119G mission after the departure of the Americans, he stated simply that "they can do it."[59/]

Early Employment - AC-119K

The AC-119K joined the 14th Special Operations Wing at the end of 1969 and by February 1970, there were 18 "Stinger" gunships in Southeast Asia. Two aircraft were lost in the spring of 1970 at Da Nang AB to equipment malfunction. The AC-119K was similar to the "Shadow" gunship, but its additional equipment gave it added capabilities. The configuration of the AC-119K "Stinger" gunship is portrayed in the following chart:

AC-119K CONFIGURATION CHART

Analog Computer

Advanced Analog Computer - Installed in February 1971

Forward-Looking Radar (APQ-136)

Beacon Tracking Radar (AN/APQ 133) - Removed December 1970

Forward-Looking Infrared (FLIR) - AAD-4

Night Observation Sight

Doppler

Flare Launcher

20 KW Illuminator

ECM Warning Device - (APQ 25/26)

7.62mm Guns

20mm Guns

SOURCE: Commando Hunt V, May 1971

The addition of two auxiliary J-85 jet engines increased the capability of the aircraft. The maximum takeoff weight for the AC-119G series was 64,000 lbs. but the additional equipment of the AC-119K brought its operational takeoff weight up to 80,400 lbs.; hence, the need for more power. Additionally, the jet engines allowed the AC-119K series to operate in mountainous areas with greater survivability than the two-engine AC-119G aircraft.

Because of the AC-119Ks' advanced sensors and increased armament, the aircraft's mission was more oriented toward armed reconnaissance and

STINGER COMPONENTS AND CHARACTERISTICS

ACFT	AC-119K
MISSION	ARMED RECCE/INTERDICTION
AREA/TARGET	IN-COUNTRY/TROOPS IN CONTACT, MOVERS, ETC. AND OUT-COUNTRY/TRUCKS, LOCS
ARMAMENT	4 x 7.72mm MINIGUNS FAST: 6,000 RDS/MIN SLOW: 3,000 RDS/MIN 2 x 20mm CANNON 2,500 RDS/MIN
ARMOR	2,000 LBS
ORDNANCE	21,500 RDS 7.62mm 3,000 RDS 20mm
FIRE CONTROL	COMPUTERIZED FCS, INCORPORATING FULLY AUTO, AUTO, MANUAL FIRING, OFF-SET CAPABLE
TGT ACQ (SENSORS	NIGHT OBSERVATION SIGHT (NOS) INFRARED
ILLUMINATION	ILLUMINATOR 1.5 MILLION CANDLEPOWER PENCIL BEAM (20 KW). 24 FLARES DISPENSED FROM LAUNCHER
REACTION AIRSPEE	180K+TAS
ALTITUDE	3,500 FT AGL (OPTIMUM)
FUEL DURATION	5+00
TURNAROUND	30 MIN
ESCORTS	NONE
AIRCREW	2 PILOTS 3 NAV, TABLE NAV, NOS OPS, RADAR/IR OPR 1 ILLUM OPR 3 GUNNERS 1 FLT ENGINEER
ONE ENGINE OUT	500 FPM CLIMB

FIGURE 11

AC-119K "Stinger" Gunship: Note
20mm Cannon and J-85 Jet Engines

Figure 12

AC-119K "Stinger" Gunship: ~~Interior~~ *NOTE 40MM CANNON*

Figure 13

truck killing than that of the AC-119G. The aircraft was eventually settled into two operating locations. AC-119Ks were equally distributed between Da Nang AB, RVN, and Nakhon Phanom RTAFB, Thailand,in April 1971. The flight at Da Nang was primarily concerned with armed reconnaissance in the Steel Tiger region of Laos with a secondary mission of providing close air support for troops in contact in Military Region 1.[60/] The flight at Nakhon Phanom was primarily oriented toward close air support for troops in contact in the Barrel Roll region of Laos with a secondary mission of armed reconnaissance in the Plaine des Jarres.[61/] The aircraft were extremely effective in both of these missions.

The diverse operating locations and the organizational support caused some difficulty for the AC-119K personnel. The flight at Nakhon Phanom for example, was placed under the 56th Special Operations Wing (Nakhon Phanom) for support. The flight was assigned to the 18th Special Operations Squadron at Phan Rang, however, and flew combat missions directed by 7AF. This complex situation required excessive coordination to reconcile the areas of support, command and control, and administration. Despite this problem, the aircrews were able to effectively employ the AC-119K and perform their mission as required.[62/]

Armed Reconnaissance

The AC-119K was extremely effective as a truck killer, but care had to be taken to avoid areas of heavy AAA concentration. As with other gunships, the AC-119K's relatively slow speed and predictable attack pattern made it vulnerable to AAA. In areas where there was no enemy

AAA, the AC-119Ks used 5,500 feet AGL as a working altitude and in areas with AAA present, 7,000 feet AGL was used.[63/]

Despite the necessity of avoiding areas of heavy AAA concentration in Laos, the AC-119K was able to produce significant results in its armed reconnaissance role. During the last six months of 1970, the Stingers destroyed 275 vehicles and damaged another 275.[64/] On 16 December, an AC-119K set the 1970 record for total trucks destroyed or damaged by all types of gunships. This record for one mission was 29 trucks destroyed and six damaged. During this same period they also destroyed 279 sampans and damaged 64.[65/] These figures are subject to qualification, however, for the time period covers only a portion of the dry season in Laos. Enemy truck traffic was generally low during the wet season and high during the dry season. The Stinger gunships were also often withdrawn from truck hunting activity to provide close air support for troops in contact; support of TICs accounted for 329 confirmed enemy KBA.[66/]

Normal working altitude for TIC targets was 3,500 feet AGL.[67/] This enabled the AC-119Ks to shoot accurately with both the 20mm cannon and 7.62mm miniguns and be relatively safe from small arms fire. Heavy automatic weapons (12.7mm and 14.5mm) were not often encountered in a TIC situation and heavy AAA was rarely present.[68/]

A mix of 20mm API/HEI was introduced on an experimental basis to see if this would enhance the AC-119K's truck killing capability. Hq PACAF concluded that the initial returns were inconclusive, but Stinger crew

31

members felt otherwise. On 28 February 1971, Stinger 04 destroyed eight PT-76 tanks using the 20mm API/HEI mix while operating in support of Lam Son 719. The ground commander on the scene confirmed that all eight tanks were completely destroyed.[69/] In addition, AC-119K aircraft destroyed or damaged 1,845 vehicles during the first three months of 1971.[70/] A revision of official opinion was clearly in order and one was soon forthcoming. It was acknowledged that "there is now very definite evidence that the ammo mix results in appreciably increased effectiveness."[71/] Consequently, the 20mm API/HEI mix became standard for all AC-119K ordnance loads.

Observations

The AC-119G was an extremely useful weapon system and it performed a variety of missions above and beyond its primary mission of close air support for troops in contact. It proved invaluable for convoy escort and armed reconnaissance in Cambodia and it was fortunate that a permissive environment existed to enable it to perform such missions during the day, as well as during the hours of darkness. The use of 7.62mm API ammunition greatly enhanced the combat effectiveness of the AC-119G, for it enabled the aircraft to destroy vehicles and watercraft which had previously been invulnerable to 7.62mm ball ammunition. The 7.62 API also enabled the pilot to precisely adjust his fire on each successive firing pass. It was unfortunate that more of this ammunition was not available.

The transfer of the AC-119G aircraft and mission from the 17th SOS (USAF) to the 819th CS (VNAF) was being accomplished as programmed. Certain

32

problem areas such as VNAF crew coordination, language difficulties and lack of experience in certain crew positions became readily apparent and efforts were made to find workable solutions.

The AC-119K's expanded capability was put to good use in the Steel Tiger and Barrel Roll regions of Laos. The aircraft was an excellent truck killer and proved equally useful in providing close air support for troops in contact. The aircraft's effectiveness as a truck killer was enhanced by using a 20mm API/HEI mix rather than straight 20mm HEI ammunition.

A large turnover of flight crew and maintenance personnel took place at the end of 1970 and this caused the 18th SOS considerable difficulty in providing meaningful training for new replacements and at the same time maintaining a high level of combat effectiveness on operational missions.[72] Nevertheless, the AC-119K Stinger gunship performed all assigned missions in an exemplary manner, with primary emphasis placed upon armed reconnaissance and interdiction.

CHAPTER III

AC-130 COMBAT OPERATIONS

Early Employment

The introduction of the AC-130A "Spectre" has been discussed in
a previous CHECO Report, "The Role of USAF Gunships in Southeast Asia."
The Spectre gunship provided a night close air support capability far
superior to that of previous gunships, and it was also admirably suited
for interdiction operations against enemy supply routes.[73] Increased
firepower in the form of 20mm cannon and advanced night and all-weather
sensors increased its effectiveness and expanded its mission capability.[74]

After a highly successful combat evaluation in early 1968, the AC-
130 flew interdiction and strike missions against enemy truck traffic
in Laos. On 14 June 1968, General Momyer, Commander 7AF, ordered the
aircraft to Tan Son Nhut Airfield, RVN, to help counter the anticipated
third phase of the enemy's Tet offensive. The AC-130 performed a wide
variety of missions in RVN, but its activities were primarily directed
toward the interdiction of enemy sampan and vehicular traffic. The AC-130's
increased firepower and advanced sensors clearly demonstrated that it was
far superior to the AC-47 Spooky and AC-119G Shadow gunships.

The evaluation phases and the conditional status of the AC-130
were terminated in late 1968 and the 16th Special Operations Squadron
was organized at Ubon RTAFB, Thailand.[75] As production aircraft arrived
(initially, four in November and December 1968), the squadron immediately

34

began flying interdiction missions against enemy truck traffic in Laos, and the original Spectre aircraft was returned to Ling Tempco Vought for alteration to a standard production model.[76/]

A sequence of operational priorities was established for the AC-130, and these priorities clearly indicated the versatility and effectiveness of the weapon system:[77/]

Priority 1: Night interdiction and armed reconnaissance to destroy wheeled or tracked vehicular traffic on roads and sampans on waterways.

Priority 2: Night interdiction of targets which have been bombed and then hit with fire suppression missions.

Priority 3: Close fire support of U.S. and friendly military installations including forts, outposts and strategic towns, and cities.

Priority 4: Search and Rescue support.

Priority 5: Offset firing in support of troops in contact utilizing aircraft radar and ground beacons.

Priority 6: Perform daylight armed escort of road and offshore convoys.

Priority 7: Harassment and interdiction missions.

The primary mission of the AC-130 was night interdiction and armed reconnaissance with less emphasis on close air support of troops in contact. Battle damage assessments indicated that the aircraft was extremely effective in its primary mission. As of March 1969, the 16th SOS had three AC-130s (the original Spectre having returned to CONUS) and a UE authorization of eight aircraft.

AC-130A "Spectre" Gunship

Figure 14

SPECTRE DEBUT

BATTLE DAMAGE ASSESSMENT 31 JAN 69 - 31 MAR 69

ITEM	JAN	FEB	MAR	TOTAL
Missions Fragged	65	81	99	245
Missions Flown	63	73	89	225
Air Aborts	3	7	4	14
Ground Aborts	2	3	11	16
Trucks Sighted	542	618	693	1,853
Trucks Destroyed	105	210	292	607
Trucks Damaged	115	138	98	351
Trucks RNO	140	181	226	547
Boats Sighted	1	22	0	23
Boats Destroyed	1	10	0	11
Troops in Contact	8	2	3	13
Helicopters Sighted	0	0	4	4
Helicopters Destroyed	0	0	0	0
Secondary Fires	126	421	630	1,177
Secondary Explosions	182	514	805	1,501

SOURCE: CHECO Report: Role of USAF Gunships in SEA, 30 August 1969

The introduction of the AC-130 to the combat environment of South-east Asia was not without problems. As was the case with earlier gunships, Spectre encountered significant difficulty with enemy ground fire. The 37mm and 57mm AAA were a particularly dangerous threat to the AC-130 and significant numbers of both could be expected wherever there was enemy truck traffic. The AC-130 was not designed to engage in duels with enemy AAA forces, but the aircrews were required to contend with this threat to get at the trucks. The AC-130 began taking numerous hits as the enemy increased the scope and intensity of his AAA efforts. On 24 May 1969, an AC-130 sustained two hits from 37mm AAA and was subsequently destroyed during an emergency landing attempt.

The Spectre gunship's relatively slow airspeed and predictable attack pattern (left hand orbit) were the prime factors in the aircraft's survivability problem.[78/] These operational parameters were not subject to change, so effective means were devised to protect the aircraft from heavy AAA fire. F-4 aircraft were assigned to fly armed escort and flak suppression missions for AC-130 gunships.[79/] The F-4s were effective in the gun-killing role, and the AC-130s were able to operate in areas heretofore prohibitive because of intense enemy AAA fire. The enemy quickly adjusted his AAA tactics and increased the volume of his fire in an attempt to counter the AC-130/F-4 team tactic, but the gunships were able to continue operations in areas of relatively high AAA threat in spite of these efforts.

Role of Technology

Technology played a significant role in the spectacular debut of the AC-130, and several important subsystems were central to the aircraft's combat effectiveness.[80/] The success or failure of the mission

AC-130: 20mm Cannon and 7.62mm Miniguns

Figure 15

TRUCK, 6x6, ZIL-157

One of the Principal Trucks used by NVA Forces

Figure 16

depended directly on the AC-130's sensors and other associated equipment; trucks that could not be located could not be destroyed.

The LORAN navigation set, AN/ARN-92C/D was an essential part of the AC-130's electronic inventory. It consisted of a medium range (250 to 500 nautical miles) LORAN D navigation system capable of receiving LORAN C ground station signals for long range (1,500 nautical miles) navigation. The LORAN D system converted time differences (TDs) between master and slave LORAN stations into position data in terms of either latitude and longitude, Universal Transverse Mercator (UTM) grid system coordinates, or range and bearing coordinates to .01 minutes, UTMs to the nearest 10 meters, range to .01 miles and bearings to .01 minutes.

The forward looking infrared (FLIR) system consisted of a mechanical and optical scanner, infrared detectors, associated electronics packages and a CRT display monitor. This system provided a day/night viewing capability under any or all conditions of target illumination. The FLIR was in essence, a heat sensing and detection device which displayed target information based upon the differential heat emitting qualities of various surface materials. Since all objects and materials radiate heat to some extent, everything within the field of view of the IR sensing elements was portrayed on the display monitor. Especially hot objects or materials (e.g., fires, vehicle engines, and vehicle surfaces) were readily detected, although detection range varied with weather conditions, humidity and the amount of foliage in the area of interest. The

AAD-4 FLIR was installed in the Update AC-130s. The AAD-6 FLIR in the PAVE PRONTO aircraft had improved detectors which made for a clearer, sharper display of target information.

The AC-130 was also equipped with the APQ-133 radar which was intended to detect, acquire and track the signal from a small X-band beacon transponder carried by friendly ground troops. The primary function of this equipment was to provide target offset information from given ground reference point (namely, ground troop location). The aircraft was to be guided to the target area by the beacon signal, and target offset information fed into the computer when the proper orbit was established about the beacon. Because of various problems, the APQ-133 was seldom used during AC-130 missions.[81]

The AN/AVG-2 Night Observation Device (NOD) was an electronically stabilized image light intensifier (40,000 to 1) used for observation of ground targets at night. This direct viewing device amplified reflected light (moonlight, starlight, and sky glow) to produce a magnified, visible image through the eyepiece. When the available light was sufficient, as on dark overcast nights, covert or overt augmentation could be provided by an illuminator. The illuminator was mounted on the cargo ramp and was steerable in azimuth and elevation from a remote position. It had a 40 kw output, and a selector switch permitted the operator to select either visible light or infrared.[82]

The AN/AWG-13 analog computer received inputs from the NOD, FLIR and beacon tracking radar of the aircraft, and it integrated the inputs from these sensors to establish a line of sight to a designated point. It corrected the fire control equations for in-flight wind, true airspeed and altitude. The computer then provided the interface which allowed an attack to be made with a preselected sensor or combination of sensors. [83]

The aforementioned items of equipment were standard on the basic AC-130A or "Plain Jane" aircraft through 1970. AC-130A #54-0490 was specially modified to serve as a test bed for new and advanced equipment. Known as "Surprise Package," this aircraft is discussed in detail in another chapter, but it deserves mention at this point since it had a significant impact on the entire Spectre gunship inventory. The "Surprise Package" aircraft was introduced during the Commando Hunt III Campaign (November 1969 through April 1970).

The AC-130, with its sophisticated sensing equipment, performed its truck killing mission in an outstanding manner during the Commando Hunt III Campaign. The "Surprise Package" aircraft produced spectacular results, and it was termed "the most effective weapon system used in Commando Hunt III for killing trucks." [84] The following statistics reflect the effectiveness of both types of AC-130s against trucks from 1 November 1969 to 30 April 1970:

40

AIRCRAFT EFFECTIVENESS: STEEL TIGER REGION

Aircraft	Trucks D/D	Sorties Attacking Trucks	Trucks Struck	Trucks D/D Sortie	Trucks D/D vs. Trucks Struck
Surprise Pkg	822	112	1104	7.34	.74
Other AC-130	2562	591	4742	4.34	.54
AC-123	440	141	854	3.12	.52
AC-119	987	435	2005	2.27	.49
A-6	977	1486	2708	.66	.36
A-1	1271	2332	4602	.55	.28
A-7	959	3147	3866	.30	.25
F-4	1576	6310	11178	.25	.14
A-4	245	1223	1446	.20	.17
TOTAL	9839	15777	32505	.62	.30

SOURCE: Commando Hunt III, May 1970   DOA 70-300

The advent of the wet season and the termination of the Commando Hunt III Campaign signaled a significant decrease in the scope and intensity of AC-130 combat operations. Enemy truck traffic slowed considerably, and the AC-130 sensors were unable to penetrate the low undercast cloud conditions often associated with the monsoon.

Five AC-130 aircraft were returned to the United States for modifications to include installation of a Black Crow sensor and two 40mm cannons. Upon their return from modification, these aircraft

ARMED RECONNAISSANCE METHODS
ON ROAD NETWORKS

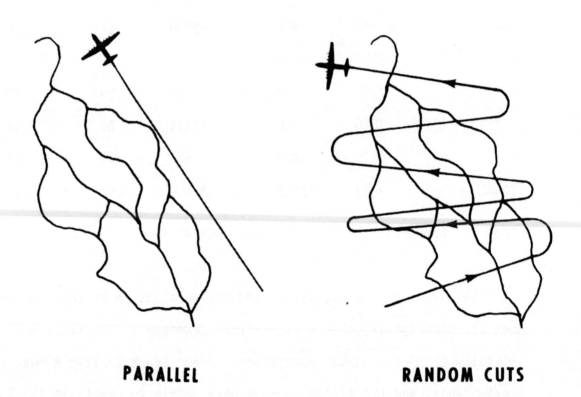

PARALLEL   RANDOM CUTS

Figure 17

TRENDS IN AIRCRAFT EFFECTIVENESS AGAINST TRUCKS

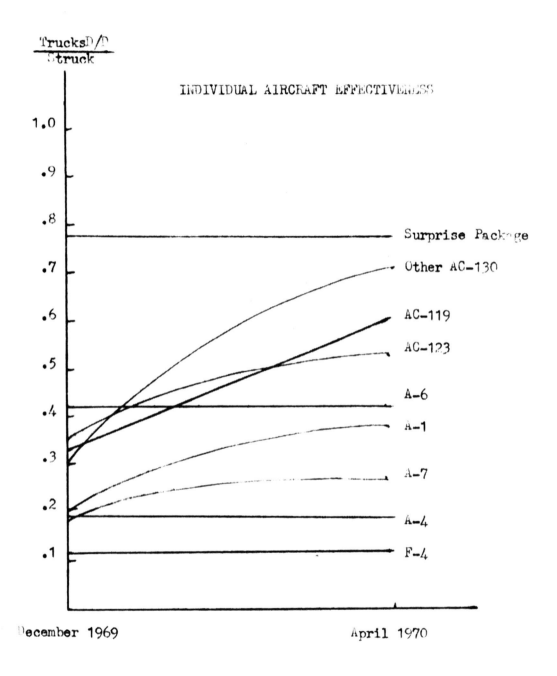

SOURCE: Commando Hunt III, May 1970
          DOA 70-300

FIGURE 17a

40mm Guns Mounted on AC-130 Spectre Gunship

Figure 18

AC-130 Spectre Gunship: interior

Figure 19

were designated "Update" AC-130s. In the meantime, new AC-130A aircraft had arrived from the United States. These aircraft, designated
"PAVE PRONTO" were patterned after the highly successful "Surprise
Package" aircraft, and they arrived in time for the 1970-1971 dry
season in Laos. The first PAVE PRONTO aircraft flew in combat on
22 November 1970.$\frac{85/}{}$

The "Surprise Package" retained its role as a test bed for continued development of specialized tactics and techniques. Nevertheless,
this unique aircraft also retained its primary role as a truck killer,
flying its first combat mission during the Commando Hunt V Campaign
on 25 October 1970.$\frac{86/}{}$

The AC-130 gunship forces available for the 1970-1971 dry season
was larger than in previous years. By March 1971, there were 12 aircraft available for combat operations, and all were equipped with 40mm
guns and improved sensors. Figure 20 lists the armament and sensors
carried on the different configurations of the AC-130 employed during
the 1970-1971 dry season.

Operational Environment

The 1970-1971 dry season witnessed intensified activity on the
part of the AC-130 force, and had brought the effectiveness and problems
of gunships into sharp focus. The AC-130 had compiled an impressive
record during its brief history of combat operations. (See Figure 21.)
Hq 7AF evaluated AC-130 operations as "superb in every respect, and there

42

are no ifs, ands, or buts about this evaluation here or anywhere else."[87/]

But there was doubt in some quarters regarding the wisdom of allocating further resources to this unique but effective weapon system. General Momyer, TAC Commander, sent the following message to higher headquarters on 21 January 1970:[88/]

> *We should freeze the AC-130 at its present capability and pursue an approach which gives us a better high speed capability to meet an expanded enemy posture... I therefore am opposed to further diversion of our airlift resources to these other roles.*

The AC-130 also encountered significant problems in its operational environment. The enemy tried to intensify his AAA capability to such an extent that Spectre gunships would either be shot down or driven from the skies over Laos. This was a sound enemy tactic for basic gunship doctrine clearly revealed certain weaknesses of lateral firing aircraft which were capable of being exploited by a resourceful and determined enemy.[89/]

> *Limitations evolving from their relatively slow speeds and the necessity to operate at low altitude dictate that air superiority must exist and areas of heavy automatic weapons and/or antiaircraft artillery (AAA) fire must be avoided.*

The AC-130 was indeed vulnerable to heavy concentrations of AAA fire, but F-4 escorts for flak suppression helped reduce this danger and the installation of 40mm guns gave the AC-130 a greater target stand-off capability.[90/*] Certain sky conditions increased the aircraft's

* See APPENDIX M.

AC-130 EQUIPMENT CONFIGURATION (1970-1971)

EQUIPMENT	SURPRISE PACKAGE	PAVE PRONTO	UPDATE
Digital Computer	X		
Analog Computer	Backup Only	X	X
Radar W/MTI	X	X	X
FLIR	AAD-4 (MOD)	AAD-6	AAD-4
Laser Range Designator	X		
Laser Target Designator	X	X	X
LLLTV	X	X	
Helmet Sight	X		
BLACK CROW	X	X	X
Night Observation Device (NOD)			X
LORAN/Doppler	X	X	X
Inertial Nav/Target System	X		
Flare Launcher	X		X
2 KW Illuminator	X	X	X
ECM Warning and Jammer	X	X	X
Video Tape Recorders	X	X	X
7.62mm Miniguns	TWO HOUR INSTALLATION CAPABILITY		
20mm Guns (2)	X	X	X
40mm Guns (2)	X	X	X

SOURCE: Commando Hunt V, May 1971,
Hq 7th AF

FIGURE 20

SPECTRE RESULTS: 1 MAY 1969-31 MARCH 1970

	MAY	JUN	JUL	AUG	SEP	OCT	NOV	DEC	JAN	FEB	MAR
MISSIONS FRAGGED	147	105	93	79	80	94	159	229	256	233	265
MISSIONS FLOWN	120	85	72	70	78	91	148	206	229	210	243
FLIGHT TIME	480.9	358.5	371.5	321.4	373.6	435.4	524.0	930.8	987.2	888.5	1014.7
AIR ABORTS	3	3	5	3	2	0	3	6	4	10	11
GROUND ABORTS	8	4	5	0	0	3	5	6	10	10	7
CANCELLATIONS	16	13	11	6	0	0	3	11	13	3	4
TRUCKS DESTROYED	427	46	22	20	16	44	227	241	581	734	508
TRUCKS DAMAGED	120	21	7	8	21	40	94	163	249	208	239
TRUCKS RNO	247	45	14	18	42	147	332	394	488	329	406
SECONDARY EXP.	1,050	900	603	150	108	140	757	355	631	971	999
SECONDARY FIRES	462	98	101	55	69	95	390	367	685	739	630
BOATS DESTROYED	4	8	1	1	1	0	0	0	0	0	3
TIC MISSIONS	0	0	12	2	12	0	0	0	1	0	0
KBA (CONF.)	0	0	290	RNO	505	0	0	0	RNO	0	0
AAA RECEIVED*	24,702	1,261	402	381	363	2,468	6,900	14,867	37,970	36,609	48,439

* 57mm, 37mm, 23mm, ZPU, and Rockets

SOURCE: 16th SOS History

FIGURE 21

AAA WEAPONS THREAT

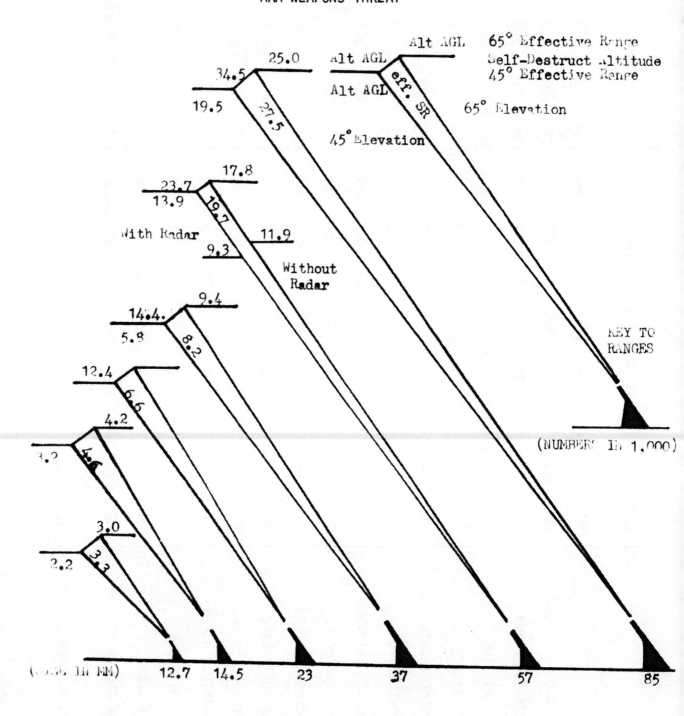

SOURCE: DIO, Hq 7AF

FIGURE 22

vulnerability to AAA fire. During the period of a full moon the aircraft was clearly visible to enemy gunners if it were operating under an overcast and such conditions elicited an accurate hail of AAA fire. Even a quarter moon with a high thin overcast silhouetted the AC-130 like "a fly on a movie screen."[91/] Such was the case on 22 April 1970, when AC-130 #54-1625 was lost to hostile fire while conducting armed reconnaissance over Laos. Ten of the crew members are listed as missing in action and one man was recovered.[92/]

Undercast sky conditions also presented a problem, for the pilot had less reaction time to avoid enemy fire. Standard flak evasion technique was to position a scanner on the right side of the aircraft and the illuminator operator hanging out over the cargo ramp in the rear and secured to the aircraft by cables. These scanners reported all AAA reactions to the pilot as either inaccurate, which required no evasive action, or they called for a "break" or a "hard break" to the right or left to avoid accurate fire. When the scanner called for a break, the pilot immediately put the aircraft into a 60° bank in the indicated direction. When a hard break was required, a 90° bank was used.

Undercast sky conditions were present on 25 January 1971 when AC-130 #54-1623 sustained a direct hit from a 37mm shell in #1 engine.[93/] The aircraft commander was able to return to base safely, but such incidents illustrated the gravity of the AAA threat to the AC-130.

44

Surface-to-Air Missiles (SAMs) constituted an even greater danger to the AC-130. This aircraft could not be expected to operate in a confirmed SAM environment. Nevertheless, Spectre crews experienced five incidents involving SAM launches against their aircraft, and the combined threat of SAMs and radar controlled AAA guns was potentially disastrous for the AC-130. Official cognizance had been taken of this potential threat since the early days of Spectre combat operations. [94/]

> AC-130s must operate in a permissive environment
> and this weapon system cannot survive in heavy
> enemy AAA fire or SAM threat areas. This includes
> radar controlled weapons.

When a SAM launch was detected by the Black Crow operator, the illuminator operator or the scanner, that crewmember immediately informed the crew of the launch. The illuminator operator then watched the missile approach the aircraft and when he judged impact to be imminent, he requested the pilot to dive. In the interim, the table navigator obtained a fix and advised the pilot of the minimum altitude to which he could dive. This tactic worked against SAMs, but the diving maneuver also increased the threat from AAA.

The enemy worked diligently to improve his AAA capability, and the threat to the Spectre gunships increased with the advent of each dry season. [95/] The increased enemy effort was obvious to the AC-130 aircrews, for from 1969 to 1970, there was a 155 percent increase in enemy AAA reactions. [96/] One AC-130 aircrew member gave the following assessment of the problem: [97/]

AC-130 Battle Damage: Aircraft #55-0044, 23 January 1971

Figure 23

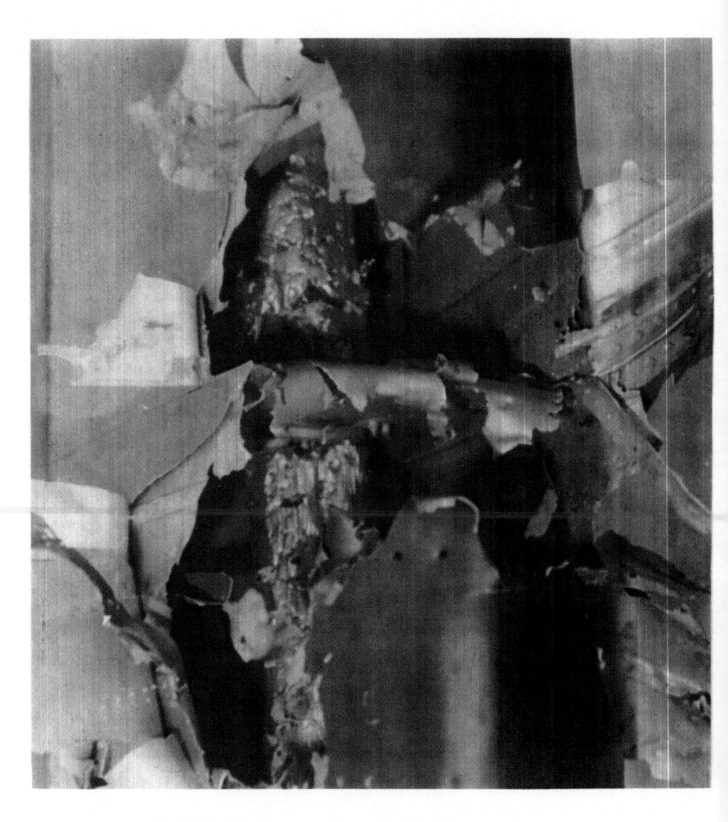

AC-130 Battle Damage: Aircraft #55-490, 3 May 1971

Figure 24

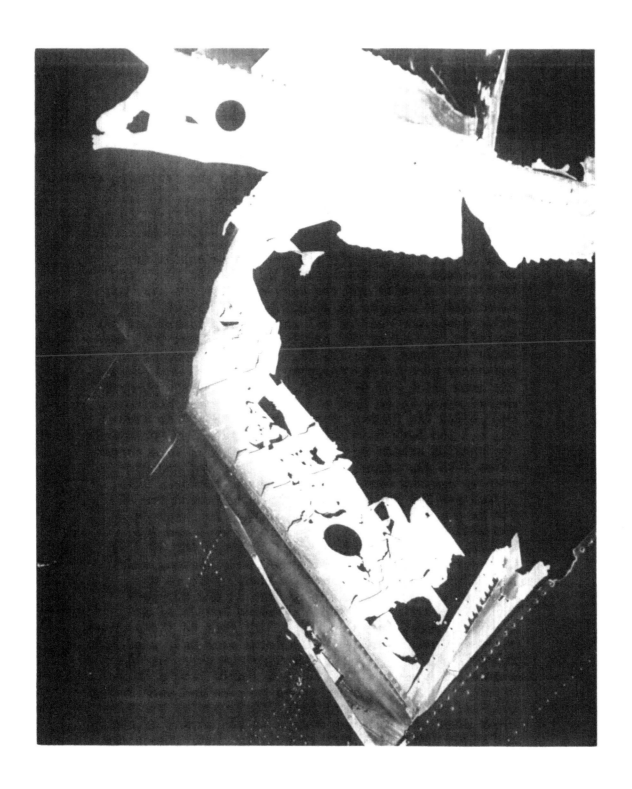

AC-130 Battle Damage: Aircraft #55-046, 9 May 1971

Figure 25

*The most significant problem affecting the AC-130
operation has been the increasing difficulty of
operating in an almost untenable night AAA environment.*

An official assessment of the situation provided the following description of AC-130 combat operations and problems: 98/

*Crew duties are specific and crew coordination is
an absolute must. The copilot adjusts the power and
monitors and calls out the bank angle as the aircraft
commander is engaged in tracking the gunsight. The
table navigator handles all navigation, determines the
position, specifies the altitude to be flown MSL, and
calls the turns. The TV, IR, and Black Crow sensor
operators pick up the targets, track them, and advise
the crew which one to attack. Meanwhile, the gunners
are standing by to load the guns, clear malfunctions
and police the brass. Concurrently, the IO is lean-
ing out the back door observing AAA fire and recommend-
ing evasive action to be taken if the flak is a threat.
Three F-4s fly escort for each gunship and are con-
stantly cycling back and forth to the tanker. This
allows one F-4 to always be above and behind the AC-
130 in a position to roll in for flak suppression.
The whole scheme works out amazingly well and the
results are rather impressive. Although the AC-130s
have sustained some battle damage this season, only
one aircrew member has been wounded. This is a
remarkable record considering that in the two-week
period...about two to three thousand rounds of AAA
fire were received every night. If this is the average,
lightning arithmetic would indicate over half a million
rounds have been fired at the Spectres this hunting
season...The reason for this remarkable record is
superior crew discipline, sound tactics and outstanding
professionalism. The one thing that worries the aircrews about the next dry season is the threat of SAM
and radar controlled AAA, especially 57mm. These two
weapons plus an eventual all-weather road system in
Laos will probably give the initiative back to the
enemy. The aircrew consensus seemed to be: "What
the heck are we doing about these potential threats."*

Despite the steadily increasing enemy AAA effort, the Spectre gunships continued their excellent performance during the 1970-71 dry season in Laos. On 14 January 1971, an AC-130 crew established a new squadron record for trucks destroyed on a single mission. Spending three hours in the target area, Spectre 04 destroyed 58 trucks and damaged seven.[99/] The escort fighter aircraft destroyed an additional seven trucks and damaged 10. This was an outstanding mission, but it could not be termed a typical AC-130 performance. In this particular instance conditions were ideal; the crew was highly experienced and all sensors were operating efficiently.

New advanced equipment played an important role in the increased effectiveness of the Spectre gunships. The AC-130 was extremely useful in effecting the accurate delivery of Laser Guided Bombs (LGB). PAVE SWORD missions once again teamed the AC-130 with the F-4 to destroy enemy resources. On 3 February 1971, Spectre 12 and its F-4 escort successfully destroyed a 37mm gun using a Laser Guided Bomb.[100/] This was the first time the AC-130 gunship employed this system under actual combat conditions. On 19 February 1971, the effectiveness of the PAVE SWORD concept was again demonstrated when a Spectre aircraft used laser guidance and the F-4 expended four LGBs to destroy two trucks.[101/] The AC-130 was then diverted to another target requiring close air support for troops in contact. Few weapon systems could boast equal versatility.

The Black Crow also greatly enhanced the AC-130's combat effectiveness. It was a valuable sensor and the only one that could penetrate

Photo Taken Immediatley After AF-130 Strike on Truck Convoy

Figure 26

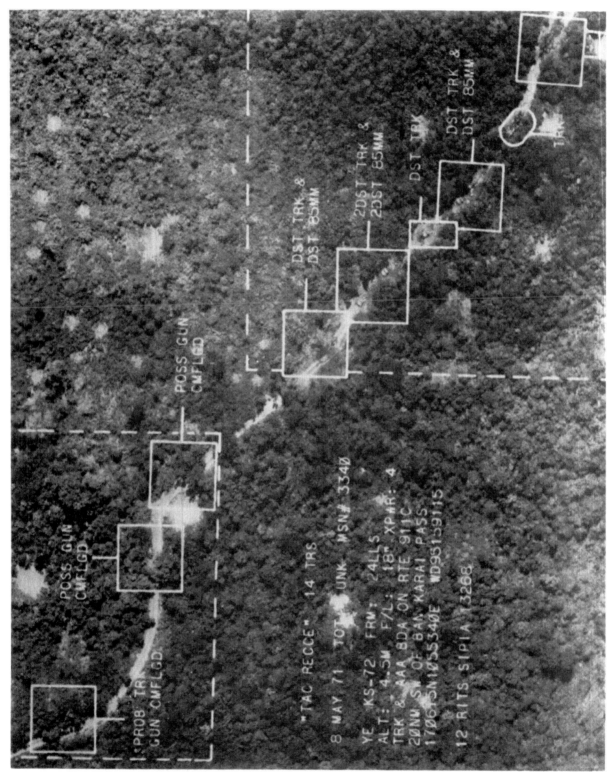

AC-130 Poststike Results Confirmed by Photo Interpretation

Figure 27

cloud cover. The Black Crow microwave equipment functioned primarily as a target acquisition sensor to provide initial information on targets for the other sensors. After the aircraft had established its orbit, the LLLTV and FLIR could look in the direction of the acquired target for lock-on and subsequent firing of the 40mm and 20mm guns. The Black Crow consistently detected numerous trucks through foliage and clouds, and also detected trucks that escaped initial detection by the other sensors. This sensor's capability was somewhat limited, however, because it could detect a truck only if the engine was operating and it was only marginally effective in detecting diesel engines.

SPECTRE DETECTION AND STRIKE ANALYSIS
1 NOV 70 - 30 APR 71

Sensor Used for Initial Sighting			Sensor Used for Firing		
BC	NOD/TV	IR	BC	NOD/TV	IR
10,449	1872	5013	32	5548	9519
60.39%	10.78%	28.83%	0.32%	36.11%	63.57%

Total Sighted	Total Attached	Total D/D
17,384	15,096	10,319/2733-13,052

86.15% of Total Sighted were attacked
86.69% of Total Attacked were D/D
75.14% of Total Sighted were D/D
8.4 trucks destroyed/damaged per sortie

SOURCE: 16SOS Briefing Folder, May 1971

The Black Crow also found useful employment supporting troops in contact. PAVE MACE was the code name for a beacon tracking system that utilized a ground beacon in conjunction with the Black Crow sensor for firing during close air support missions. The TEMIG/Coded Beacon was installed in the hand held RT-10 radio chassis and had a battery life of approximately eight hours. This piece of equipment was designed to be as foolproof as possible and was engineered for use by people unable to read any language or speak English.[102] This beacon was also specifically designed to be used in all visibility conditions and without any other means of communication between the aircraft and the man on the ground.[103]

When the beacon was activated, it transmitted coded signals to the aircraft which included location, beacon identifier, range to target, bearing to target and type of target.[104] The decoder in the AC-130 deciphered the beacon signal and displayed a series of four groups of four digit numbers on the Black Crow console which represented, in turn, the beacon identifier, range to target, bearing to target and type of target. The Black Crow operator passed this information to the table navigator who, in turn, inserted the appropriate numbers into the fire control computer. The signal power output of the beacon was designed to facilitate its detection by the Black Crow equipment at a range of 10 to 15 nautical miles through triple canopy jungle foliage, and in the open the equipment detection range was 50 nautical miles.[105]

An AC-130 equipped with PAVE MACE equipment could navigate to the general target area, acquire the beacon and assimilate the appropriate offset data and then fire on the target without ever communicating with the friendly forces or even seeing the ground. This sophisticated equipment was employed under actual combat conditions and it performed admirably. On 2 June 1971, an AC-130 worked with a Forward Air Guide (FAG), call sign Hunter, at Lima Site 32 located in the Barrel Roll region of Laos. The existing weather consisted of a 2,000-foot overcast, and the AC-130 stayed above the cloud deck, working targets varying in range from 400 to 1,000 meters from the friendly position.[106/] The FAC corroborated the firing passes with oral confirmation of the areas struck, although this communication was not really necessary because of the nature of the PAVE MACE equipment. Hunter was obviously pleased with Spectre's performance, for his comments included "very good" and "number one" after each successive AC-130 firing pass.[107/]

The PAVE MACE equipment represented a truly phenomenal capability because it enabled delivery of accurate close air support firepower through an obstructing cloud deck. PAVE MACE was not an unqualified success, however, for there were some difficulties with the associated equipment. There would be even more if enemy forces developed a jammer/spoofer device to counter Black Crow/PAVE MACE. By June 1971, PAVE MACE missions were flown on a daily basis, as equipment became available to ground commanders and they gained confidence in its capabilities.

Another technological innovation was tested on the AC-130 by
introducing a new type of ammunition for the 40mm guns. The Misch
metal 40mm HEI ammunition was the same as the standard 40mm rounds
except that a one-eighth inch Misch* metal liner was added for
increased incendiary effect. The projectile characteristics were
not changed except for weight and amount of explosive charge. A
combat test was initiated by the 8th Tactical Fighter Wing on 21 January
1971, and the results were impressive. The aircrews generally felt that
the improved round was a more effective truck killer, for a "shot within
three or four mils would cause a truck to burn while with the standard
round even a direct hit at times would not cause a fire."[108] The
improved round caused four to five times more secondary fires and
explosions than the regular round. During the test and evaluation
period, which lasted from 21 January to 10 February 1971, it took an
average of 51 rounds of standard 40mm HEI to destroy one truck as
compared to 16 rounds per truck with the Misch metal ammunition.[109]
The 8TFW reached the following conclusion regarding the Misch metal
ammunition:[110]

> *The improved round is a considerable improvement*
> *over the standard round in all phases of the gun-*
> *ship mission. The improved round is a more effec-*
> *tive truck killer because of its larger pattern*

* A material which possesses pyrophoric capabilities (somewhat like
  flint stone).

51

*and incendiary effects. The improved round is
a better target marker than the standard round
because of its increased persistence and detect-
ability.*

The overall evaluation of the Misch metal ammunition was highly
favorable, but use of the ammunition was discontinued in April due
to shell extraction problems. There was some doubt among the aircrews, however, as to whether the extraction difficulties should have
been specifically ascribed to the Misch metal ammunition. Several
aircrew members believed that the extraction problems would have
occurred during the normal course of operations with the standard ammunition since the 40mm guns were manufactured during World War II and
were hardly designed for the manner in which they were being employed. 111/
The problem appeared to be purely technical in nature and warranted a
concerted effort to find an engineering solution, either by designing
a modern 40mm gun or modifying the Misch metal ammunition. On the
other hand, an AFATL-DLRV (Air Force Armament Laboratory, Eglin AFB,
Fl.) test of gunship fired munitions completed on 30 September 1971
indicated that the 40mm standard HEI round was twice as effective as
the 40mm improved (Misch metal) round for producing fragment damage
and leaks in POL cargo; however, the 40mm improved round was three
times more effective than the 40mm standard round for producing
fires. A combination of the two types of 40mm rounds would appear
to offer the best kill potential.

The AC-130 found new and unusual employment during Lam Son 719, the RVN forces' thrust into Laos launched during February 1971. A three division South Vietnamese force invaded Laos to interdict the enemy's major north-south route structure in the Tchepone region and destroy as many enemy supplies as possible.[112] One of the most startling developments of the operation was the deployment of an enemy tank regiment to the battle area. During the fighting, AC-130 gunships were pitted against enemy armor, and the results were impressive.

Three types of enemy tanks were employed during Lam Son 719. The PT-76 was a light, amphibious tank weighing 15.4 tons and carrying a 7.62mm machine gun mounted coaxially with the main gun. The T-34 was a medium tank weighing 35 tons when combat loaded and armed with an 85mm main gun. The larger T-54 weighed 40 tons and was armed with a 100mm main gun, one 12.7mm (.51 cal) machine gun on the turret roof and two 7.62mm machine guns, one mounted coaxially with the main gun and one mounted in the front of the hull. Most of the enemy tanks employed against RVNAF forces were PT-76s and it is believed that this was the only type struck by Spectre gunships.[113]

During Lam Son 719, AC-130 gunships attacked 28 enemy tanks, destroying 14 and damaging three.[114] The AC-130 was hardly designed to kill tanks, but it did a creditable job when directed against enemy armor. Two incidents were typical of the Spectre strikes: First, on 9 February 1971, Spectre 01 attacked a tank while under the control of Hammer FAC 89. **Expenditures** were 96 rounds of 40mm HEI and 35 rounds of 40mm Misch metal ammunition. The tank was destroyed and a mortar site was also silenced; these results were confirmed by friendly forces.[115/] The attack altitude was 9,500 feet AGL and no special tactics were employed. The tank was thought to be a PT-76. Second, on 3 March 1971, Spectre 12 attacked a tank believed to be a PT-76. A FAC confirmed one tank destroyed, and a later report by another FAC confirmed 300 KBA.[116/] No special tactics for flak evasion were used, although 1,400 rounds of ZPU fire were directed at the aircraft.[117/]

The AC-130 also turned in several outstanding performances of close air support for troops in contact. The TIC capability of the AC-130 was already well-known, but it was particularly valuable during Lam Son 719. AC-130s were able to respond very quickly to calls for close air support, since their assigned areas for armed reconnaissance either included or were immediately contiguous to the battle area of Lam Son 719.[118/] Specific body counts and accurate BDA for the AC-130s were difficult to obtain due to the confused nature of the fighting and the understandable reluctance of friendly ground forces to sally forth just to count enemy dead after an AC-130 strike. The following official comment, although rather conservative, provides an accurate description of the gunship role (including AC-119Ks) in Lam Son 719:[119/]

Gunships were utilized almost exclusively during the hours of darkness and were used mainly to interdict enemy vehicular traffic and to provide close air support at night for friendly base camps. With their high rate of firepower the gunships proved indispensable and highly effective, with a total of 50 to 60 enemy vehicles destroyed and rapid response to night troops in contact situations. Accurate BDA for gunships was usually impossible because of the nighttime environment in which they operated.

Criteria for Assessment of Effectiveness

The AC-130 continued its remarkable performance during the spring of 1971, and the aircraft's primary mission was still killing trucks. Problems developed, however, regarding the credibility of BDA relating to truck kills. Since the AC-130 was acknowledged as being the most effective weapon system for killing trucks, the controversy centered around the Spectre gunships' performance. The following message from the Tactical Air Command Liaison Officer (TACLO) to Headquarters 7AF indicated the nature and depth of the problem:[120]

AC-130 BDA is the hottest thing in the theater at this moment. Seventh Air Force is really concerned about the validity of the BDA reported by the AC-130 gunships in their truck killing operation. They stated all aircraft BDA for this hunting season indicates over 20,000 trucks destroyed or damaged to date, and if intelligence figures are correct, North Vietnam should be out of rolling stock. The trucks continue to roll however...

The AC-130 figures called into question were indeed "impressive" and warranted further scrutiny. During the first quarter of 1971 AC-130 strike results were recorded as follows:[121]

SPECTRE STRIKE ANALYSIS

	January 1971	February 1971	March 1971
Missions	301	290	338
Trucks Destroyed	1394	2126	3339
Trucks Damaged	374	564	827
Secondary Fires	784	1068	1294
Secondary Explosions	1214	1834	1001

These figures were even more impressive when it is noted that the AC-130 fleet flew only three percent of the total strike and armed reconnaissance missions flown by 7AF during that time period.[122/] Though there was little question that the AC-130 was the most effective truck killer in Southeast Asia (See Figure 28), a controversy developed as to the quantitative accuracy of the Spectre gunships' strike results.

Headquarters 7AF was also concerned with BDA credibility, and on 28 April 1971, a conference was held at Tan Son Nhut Airfield, RVN, attended by the 7AF Commander, members of his staff and representatives of the 8th TFW including several AC-130 crew members. It was concluded that the aircrews were honestly and accurately reporting BDA, but BDA criteria were questionable.[123/] The criteria being used and subsequently questioned were as follows:

AC-130 BDA CRITERIA

1. Destroyed

   a. Direct impact of 40mm projectile observed by sensors.

   b. 40mm impact causes a secondary explosion or fire.

   c. 20mm explosion causes a secondary explosion or fire.

2. Damaged

   a. 40mm impacts one mil low without fire.

   b. Direct impact of 20mm without fire.

SOURCE: Directorate of Tactical Analysis, Hq 7AF

The criteria were based upon the following definitions for destroyed and damaged trucks:

1. Destroyed Truck

   a. One no longer visible after a direct bomb hit.

   b. One observed burning with flames visible.

   c. A mass of twisted metal after strike.

   d. Generally speaking, a destroyed truck is one which rendered unusable and irreparable after a strike.

2. Damaged Truck

   a. One with parts missing such as hood, fenders, wheels, or portions of the undercarriage.

   b. Stopped and obviously unable to continue after strike

   c. Overturned with no fire or explosion.

SOURCE: 7AFR 200-14, 23 February 1970

AIRCRAFT PERFORMANCE AGAINST TRUCKS
10 OCT 70 - 30 APR 71

Fighters	A-1	A-4	A-6	A-7	F-4	F-100
Total Sorties	674	7551	3590	9581	27305	4635
Sorties Striking Trucks	24	1389	1052	2070	6708	200
Percent Striking Trucks	4	18	29	22	25	4
Trucks Struck	22	1413	1739	2476	9317	293
Trucks Damaged/Destroyed	7	396	518	703	2136	87
Damaged/Destroyed Struck Trucks	.29	.29	.49	.34	.32	.44
Damaged/Destroyed Trucks Struck	.32	.28	.30	.28	.23	.30

Special Systems	B-57G	AC-119K	AC-130
Total Sorties	1202	929	1437
Sorties Striking Trucks	840	558	1311
Percent Striking Trucks	70	60	91
Trucks Struck	2824	3128	14992
Trucks Destroyed/Damaged	1931	2400	12741
Destroyed/Damaged Struck Trucks	2.30	4.30	9.72
Destroyed/Damaged Hour on Station	2.30	2.15	3.24
Destroyed/Damaged Truck Struck	.68	.77	.85

SOURCE: Commando Hunt V, Hq 7th AF,
May 1971

FIGURE 28

There were indeed some inconsistencies involved in matching the AC-130 BDA criteria with the accepted definitions for destroyed and damaged trucks. For example, if a ZIL 157 truck loaded with bags of rice sustained a direct hit from a 40mm projectile in the truck bed, it was listed as destroyed according to the AC-130 BDA criteria when in fact the rice probably absorbed most of the 40mm blast effect and the truck was probably only damaged.

As result of the BDA conference, the AC-130 criteria was changed effective 1 May 1971. The new AC-130 BDA criteria stated that a truck had to have a secondary explosion or a sustained fire to be counted as destroyed; all other direct hits would be counted as damaged only.[124/] The 40mm "near miss" (one mil low) criterion for a damaged truck was dropped entirely.

Headquarters 7AF continued to study the problem of BDA criteria, and on 12 May 1971, a special test of AC-130 gunship munitions was conducted on an army firing range at Bien Hoa AB, RVN. The demonstration was intended to ascertain the effectiveness of AC-130 ordnance against vehicles. The targets were eight U.S. Government salvage M-35 trucks, some with engines running and two with POL on board.[125/] An AC-130 attacked the targets, employing the same tactics used against enemy vehicles and fired both standard and Misch metal 40mm ammunition as well as 20mm ammunition. All targets were hit except one and those trucks carrying POL burned.[126/] The 7AF evaluation of the test concluded that:[127/]

1. Sustained fire will destroy a truck.

2. Direct hits will result in damage ranging from a repairable hole to extensive damage.

3. Near misses will cause little or no damage to a truck; however, shell fragments will puncture the tires.

The test results and conclusions generally supported the revised AC-130 BDA criteria, and the revised criteria were judged more realistic for evaluating the aircraft's effectiveness against enemy trucks. It is interesting to note, however, that there was no substantial decline in the statistical effectiveness of the AC-130 (Trucks Destroyed or Damaged per Truck Struck) since the revision of the BDA criteria on 1 May 1971.[128/] There was a decline in the number of trucks destroyed or damaged per sortie even when adjustments were made for the quantifiable effects of weather and lower levels of truck activity with the advent of the wet season in Laos. Finally, there was a decrease in the fraction of trucks destroyed of the total destroyed and damaged as a consequence of the criteria change.[129/]

The revised AC-130 BDA criteria must be viewed within the operational context of the gunship mission. Any criteria, regardless of the statistical base, are subject to question. For example, the near miss (one mil low) criterion for a damaged truck was dropped entirely and no longer counted for purposes of "damage." The gunship munitions evaluation on 12 May 1971, corroborated this revision; but the ground was muddy at Bien Hoa on 12 May. The impact, explosion and fragmentation

effect of the 40mm projectile was thus minimized in the event of a
near miss. The ground was not always muddy on the enemy road network
in Laos, and it was conceivable that the Spectre gunships actually
damaged more trucks than those for which they were credited. Trucks
have been destroyed by secondary explosions on several occasions from
misses of three to four mils with a 40mm projectile.[130/] This would
indicate that, on occasion, 40mm near misses did cause considerable
damage to enemy trucks in Laos, even if there was no secondary explosion or fire. Such were the vagaries of statistics and criteria. The
nature of the gunship mission and the absence of significant friendly
forces in the area to corroborate gunship BDA had plagued the evaluation
of side firing weapon systems since the inception of the AC-47.

PAVE SPECTRE

The BDA controversy notwithstanding, the AC-130 remained the
most sophisticated and effective truck killer in Southeast Asia. Consequently, a decision was made to increase the number of aircraft in
the AC-130 gunship fleet and update the subsystems of those already
in active service. Six additional aircraft were programmed for addition
to the force. The AC-130E aircraft was designated PAVE SPECTRE and
were programmed for delivery to Southeast Asia not later than 1 January
1972.[131/] The update AC-130A aircraft in the active fleet were returned
to the United States for modification to the PAVE PRONTO configuration
and were scheduled for return to Southeast Asia by 1 November 1971. The
"Surprise Package" aircraft was also renovated and scheduled to return
to Southeast Asia in the PAVE PRONTO configuration by 1 October 1971.[132/]

60

Thus, the 16th Special Operations Squadron was scheduled to possess 12 updated AC-130s by 1 November 1971. The addition of the mix PAVE SPECTRE aircraft would provide the squadron with a total fleet strength of 18 aircraft by 1 January 1972. The "Surprise Package" aircraft was slated to retain its unique configuration as a test bed for continued development of specialized tactics and techniques and the testing of new equipment.

Observations

Most improvements in lateral firing weapon systems since the advent of the AC-47 enhanced truck killing capability. The AC-130 weapon system was a clear manifestation of this trend, and this aircraft was generally acknowledged as the most effective truck killer in the USAF inventory. During Commando Hunt III, the Laos interdiction campaign lasting from 1 November 1969 to 30 April 1970, AC-130 aircraft accounted for 34.3 percent of the total trucks destroyed or damaged while flying only 4.5 percent of the total sorties which were involved with attacking trucks.[133] During Commando Hunt V, the campaign in Laos spanning the time period from 10 October 1970 to 30 April 1971, the AC-130s accounted for 12,741 trucks destroyed or damaged, a figure which represented 61 percent of the total trucks destroyed or damaged by all aircraft during the entire campaign.[134] The Commando Hunt Campaigns corresponded to the northeast monsoon, or dry season in Laos, and thus spanned the periods of peak enemy truck traffic in transshipping supplies through Laos from North Vietnam to Viet Cong and North Vietnamese units in South Vietnam and Cambodia.

The AC-130's potency as a truck killer remained unchallenged. The controversy involving the truck destroyed and damaged criteria for AC-130s was resolved as well as could be expected considering the nature of the mission and the difficulty of confirming BDA. The revised criteria reflected a more realistic means of measuring the AC-130's combat effectiveness. Although most of the improvements in gunship systems since the AC-47 represented a shift away from the close air support role, the AC-130 remained one of the most effective weapon systems for close air support for troops in contact in the USAF inventory.

CHAPTER IV

"SURPRISE PACKAGE"

Development

"Surprise Package" constituted an innovation in the field of combat testing and evaluation. The "Surprise Package" was a gunship prototype test bed. It was a flying laboratory where new ideas, tactics, and hardware were tested and proved or rejected.

Construction of the Surprise Package aircraft started at Wright-Patterson AFB, Ohio, as the eighth and last standard AC-130A gunship. In August 1969, during the course of its modification, the Aeronautical Systems Division (ASD) proposed that the final configuration be altered to include a collection of new night attack sensors, navigation and targeting equipment, larger caliber guns, and a new digital fire control system computer.[135/] The development of these gunship improvement items started in mid-1968 with the Headquarters USAF Development Directive to provide more capable fire control system computer. In the case of the new sensors, the object was to provide increased detection ranges with better pointing accuracies, to provide a capability to detect and track targets under conditions where the existing gunship sensors were ineffective or were degraded (i.e., weather, jungle foliage, heavy haze, smoke, etc.) and to detect the target by means of a different target signature (i.e., a detection means unknown to the enemy). In the case of the guns and associated ammunition improvement, the goal was to provide improved terminal effects at increased accuracy and velocity at the increased distances. Since the USAF did not have a suitable air-to-ground gun developed, tested, and available for this program, AFSC installed an off-the-shelf World War II BOFORS 40mm AAA gun which was obtained from the U.S. Navy. AFSC believed that all of this new equipment would provide the AC-130A with the capability to fly at higher mission attack altitudes which, in turn, would establish greater stand-off distances. Greater stand-off ranges to the target would simultaneously create greater distances between the typical AAA site and the gunship since these gun sites were usually located adjacent to the roads and trails. Curves were computed for the 37mm and 57mm AAA, which showed the effect of increased slant ranges (or higher flight altitudes) on the probability of survival. An increase in the slant range of 7,000 feet (flight altitude of 5,500 feet AFL) to a projected slant range of 12,000 feet (flight altitude of 9,000 feet AFL) provided a significant increase in the probability of survival for either type gun at two different gun elevation angles.

At the beginning of the evaluation period, the standard AC-130A gunships were flying a mission attack altitude of 5,500 feet AGL. The Surprise Package Aircraft started operating in the theater at 8,500 feet AFL and eventually increased this to 10,500 feet AGL. An increase in altitude from 5,500 to 8,500 feet or even 10,500 feet did not necessarily imply that the gunship would be out of range of the 37mm AAA since the self-destruct slant range of the 37mm round was 14,400 feet, but the increase in altitude did give the crew a few seconds more reaction time to take the correct evasive action. This was important since the gunship's pylon turn attack geometry required the aircraft to remain in a relatively fixed area for extended periods of time. As a result, hostile gunners had the opportunity for repeated firing attacks. The primary questions to be answered were: (1) would the aircraft be able to detect, track, and hit the target at these greater stand-off ranges, and (2) would the combat evaluation period provide enough data to prove that an increase in altitude simultaneously provided an increase in the probability of survival?

The ASD proposal to build an enhanced and more survivable AC-130A gunship rather than a standard AC-130A was briefed at PACAF, 7AF, and the TFW before its eventual approval by Hq USAF.[136/] The improved aircraft was nicknamed by AFSC as the Surprise Package Aircraft, but was later identified by TAC as the Coronet Surprise Aircraft. Seventh Air Force agreed to the deployment of this nonstandard and enhanced AC-130A aircraft primarily on the basis of its alleged performance and with the following provisos:[137/]

 a. The aircraft could be deployed not later than 15 November 1969.

 b. The initial operational capability (ICC) would be 1 December 1969.

 c. The aircraft could be restored in-theater to the standard AC-130A configuration in not more than four days should it not be successful.

65

d. AFSC would provide complete support for all specialized
    subsystems at Ubon RTAFB, Thailand, including contractor
    technical services (CTS) personnel as required.

e. Initial employment in the theater would be made by a TAC/
    AFSC introduction and evaluation team which was knowledge-
    able in all aspects of the nonstandard subsystems.

The Commander, 7AF, officially endorsed the project on 12 August
1969, and Headquarters USAF authorized AFSC to proceed with the program
on 2 September 1969. Seventh Air Force subsequently agreed to a slippage
in the deployment date to 25 November 1969 in order to provide sufficient
time for the installation of the BLACK CROW subsystem and the TRIM-7
active ECM equipment before departure from CONUS. [138/] The CONUS evaluation was conducted by the TAC/AFSC introduction and evaluation team at
Eglin AFB, Florida, from 28 October 1969 to 15 November 1969. The
Surprise Package departed for Southeast Asia in a ferry configuration
(i.e., guns and special equipment stowed and the aircraft pressurized)
on 25 November 1969.

The clearest way to describe the aircraft is to compare its configuration with that of the standard AC-130A gunship aircraft (as of 30 April
1970). The following table provides this comparison. [139/] Detailed descriptions of individual subsystems may be found in TAC Report: TAC Operation Plan 132, Coronet Surprise, Draft Final Report, dated 6 March 1970.

<u>STANDARD AC-130A</u>	<u>SURPRISE PACKAGE AC-130A</u>
4 20mm M61 Gatling Guns	2 40mm Bofors Guns
4 7.62mm Miniguns	2 20mm M61 Gatling Guns

<u>SENSORS</u>

AN/AAD-4 Forward Looking Infrared (FLIR)	AN/AAD-4 FLIR
AN/AVG-2 Night Observation Device (NOD)	2 Low Light Level Television (LLLTV)
AN/APQ 133 Beacon Tracking Radar	Cameras (wide field of view and narrow field of view)
	AN/AVG-2 NOD (backup for LLLTV)
	AN/APQ 133 Beacon Tracking Radar S-Band Black Crow
	Moving Target Indicator (MTI) on AN/APQ 136 radar
	Helmet Sight

<u>NAVIGATION EQUIPMENT</u>

AN/ARN 92 LORAN C/D (as of Feb 70)	AN/ARN 92 LORAN C/D
AN/ARN 21 TACAN	AN/ARN 21 TACAN
AN/PRQ 136 Forward Looking Radar	AN/APQ 136 Forward Looking Radar
AN/APN 81 Doppler Radar	AN/APN 81 Doppler Radar
AN/ASN 7 Navigation Computer	AN/ASN 7 Navigation Computer
	Inertial Navigation/Targeting Subsystem (with LTN-51 inertial navigation system)

FIRE CONTROL SYSTEM

AN/AWG 13 Analog Fire Control
System Computer

Fire Control Display

Optical Gunsight

ID-48/ARN Indicator

Sensor and Light Angle
Display (SLAD)

Digital Fire Control System
Computer (primary system)

Prototype of Improved Analog

Fire Control System Computer
(backup for digital computer)

Fire Control Display

Optical Gunsight

ID-48/ARN Indicator

Sensor and Light Angle Display
(SLAD)

ECM AND RHAW EQUIPMENT

AN/APR 25/26 RHAW

TRIM 7 Active ECM

AN/APR 25/26 RHAW

TRIM 7 Active ECM

AN/APR 14 (temporary installation)

AN/ER 142 (temporary installation)

SPECIAL EQUIPMENT

Video/Audio Tape Recorder

Laser Target Designator (LTD)

AIRBORNE ILLUMINATION SYSTEM

AN/AVQ 8 40KW Illuminator

2KW Illuminator (servo driven
with LLLTV)

68

COMMUNICATIONS EQUIPMENT

AN/ARC-34 UHF Communications Systems

AN/ARC-34C UHF Communications System

AN/ARC-133(V) UHF Communications System

AN/ARC-133(V) UHF Communications System

VHF/FM Transceiver Set, FM-622A (two each)

UHF/FM Transceiver Set, FM-622A (two each)

VHF Command Radio, VHF101

VHF Command Radio, VHF101

HF Communications System HF-103

HF Communications System HF-103

HF Transceiver Set, 618T-2

HF Transceiver Set, 618T-2

SCHEDULED FOR INSTALLATION

*40mm Guns (Summer 1970)

HAVE AUGER Sensor Subsystem (Installation date unknown)

*2KW Illuminator (Summer 1970)

*MTI (Summer 1970)

*Improved Analog Fire Control System Computer, AN/AYK-9 (Summer 1970)

*Laser Target Designator (November 1970)

*Video/Audio Tape Recorder (November 1970)

*BLACK CROW (December 1970)

*Approved for installation in the standard AC-130As as a result of Combat ROCs and satisfactory combat evaluation in the Surprise Package Aircraft.

The most singularly effective innovation on "Surprise Package" was the addition of two 40mm cannons. These guns were standard Navy M1 40mm cannons, commonly known as the "Bofors." No modifications were made to

69

the gun or its operating mechanisms, but a specially built gun mount

was installed in the AC-130 cargo compartment along with an electrical

solenoid for triggering the gun remotely. The gun could be adjusted

in azimuth (o° to -15° from wing tip, aft) and in elevation (o° to -30°

from wing tip, down). 140/ The guns were loaded manually using standard

four-round clips. The muzzle velocity of the weapon was 2,870 feet per

second, and the firing rate was single fire or 120 rounds per minute

(selectable). Full specifications for the guns are contained in Navy

Manual NAVORD OP-3524. The effective range of the guns was far beyond

that of the AC-130's sensor tracking ranges so gun range was not a

significant factor in ordnance delivery.

The BLACK CROW represented another important technological innova-

tion found on the "Surprise Package" aircraft. The function of the

BLACK CROW was to identify and acquire target signals by means of

electrical impulses from vehicles operating with an ignition system

and to provide azimuth and elevation information regarding these targets

to the fire control computer. 141/ The BLACK CROW was an extremely ef-

fective detection device, and it was responsible for the detection of

approximately 65 percent of all "Surprise Package" targets during

Commando Hunt III. 142/

The "Surprise Package" was also equipped with an air-to-ground

Moving Target Indicator (MTI) intended to facilitate detection of moving

ground targets. The MTI was designed to detect targets concealed

by light to medium foliage, and moving at a rate of three to four miles

per hour or faster. Poor radar resolution, however, hampered its effectiveness.

The digital computer on "Surprise Package" accepted data from the
aircraft's sensors and gave the pilot the ability to fire accurately
from any airspeed, altitude or angle of bank rather than just at
certain airspeeds, altitudes and bank angles as was the case with the
AN/AWG-13 analog computer.

"Surprise Package" also incorporated an Inertial Navigation and
Targeting System that provided primary navigation information to the
navigator for precise positioning of the aircraft and to the fire
control system for use in long offset and direct-fire modes of
operation. To provide accurate targeting and navigational data, the
system incorporated a precision gyro-stabilized gimbal assembly for
reference and a computer for data computation and even programming.
The Intertial Navigational Unit was located on a pallet attached securely
to the aircraft structure.

The AN/APQ-135(V)-1 Forward Looking Radar provided the "Surprise
Package" aircraft with automatic flight control at low altitude and
also had videomapping capabilities. The Aircraft was thus able to
safely fly a contour of the earth's surface at selected terrain clear-
ances. This feature was intended to aid the aircraft in avoiding
detection by enemy radar.

The Low Light Level Television (LLLTV) constituted still another
important technological innovation in the "Surprise Package" aircraft.

It was used to detect and track targets under conditions varying from the low light levels encountered at night to the bright conditions of broad daylight. The LLLTV was extremely effective, but undercast cloud conditions negated its use.

Employment

One object of developing Surprise Package was to increase gunship aircraft survivability, particularly in the 23mm, 37mm, and 57mm AAA threat environment. The aircraft was to be employed in the same threat areas as the standard AC-130As. The aircraft was also to be escorted by F-4s for flak suppression in the same manner as the standard AC-130As. Mission attack altitudes, however, were to be at 8,500 AGL and above, rather than 5,500 AGL. A comparison of the operational performance of the Surprise Package with that of the standard AC-130As was programmed and a record was to be kept comparing the number of hits and losses incurred by both types of aircraft. It was hoped that the increased capability of the Surprise Package subsystems which were not installed on the standard AC-130As would enhance the effectiveness of lateral firing gun platforms and could subsequently be installed on other aircraft. Concurrently, the higher operating altitudes would reduce the AAA threat and increase survivability.

Evaluation

The initial evaluation period lasted from 12 December 1969 to 30 April 1970. The results of the evaluation were impressive. The

Surprise Package Aircraft strike results tabulated below were obtained
from the Mission Summary File containing the official bomb damage
assessment (BDA) listing in its most updated form. These statistics were
used in the Seventh Air Force Commando Hunt III Report, May 70, except
for those marked with an asterisk(s):

Armed Reconnaissance Sorties Flown	112
Trucks Observed	1,261
*Trucks Struck	1,086
Trucks Destroyed	604
Trucks Damaged	218
Secondary Fires Obtained	365
Secondary Explosions	774
Trucks Destroyed/Damaged Per Sortie	7.34
*Trucks Destroyed/Damaged Per Truck Struke	0.76
**57mm AAA Rounds Received	105
**37mm AAA Rounds Received	32,271
**23mm AAA Rounds Received	8,541
**Unguided Rockets Received	25
**ZPU Rounds Received	175

*Ref: 7AF (DOA) Letter, 10 June 1970, subject: Surprise Package BDA.
The data provided in this letter was used since it represented the
most current and correct data.

**Ref: 8TFW (S) PAFOP/TAC/AFSC Coronet Surprise Team 301115Z Apr 70,
subject: TAC/AFSC Coronet Surprise Weekly Activity Summary.
This weekly summary provided cumulative totals of all vital
data.

The vulnerability and survivability of any aircraft varies according to the mission and aircraft characteristics. Vulnerability was
computed as the probability that an aircraft would be hit were it
fired upon. Survivability was computed as the probability that an
aircraft would not be lost were it hit. The statistics are dependent
on the tactics and force employment used as well as aircraft

characteristics and enemy defenses. For example, the gunship statistics were influenced by the decision to restrict these aircraft to night flights in low threat areas. The aircraft vulnerability and survivability table in the Commando Hunt III Report provided data on all AC-130As including the Surprise Package. Using additional hit data received from the 8TFW and knowing the total sorties each type flew, an attempt was made to separate individual aircraft vulnerability and survivability data. The following information was produced: 143/

Aircraft Type	Different Locations Fired Upon	Hits (Including Losses)	Aircraft Losses	Aircraft Vulner- ability	Aircraft Surviv- ability
Standard AC-130As	2182	6 direct hits 1 shrapnel hit	1	.0032	0.86
Surprise Package	352	2 shrapnel hits	0	.0057	1.0

Although the figures indicated that the Surprise Package was more survivable than the standard AC-130As, the number of hits and losses is too low to represent a statistical valid sample; thus, little significance can be placed on the results. The statement that the Surprise Package was more survivable than the standard AC-130As might be better debated on qualitative terms rather than quantitative terms. For example:

    a. The AC-130As took six direct hits while the Surprise Package experienced no direct hits.

    b. The average time of flight for a 37mm round to reach the flight altitude of the Surprise Package was approximately 8-9 seconds (8,500 feet AGL) while the

74

time to reach the altitude of the standard AC-130As was approximately five seconds (5,500 feet AGL).

c. Because of the difference in the flight altitudes, the enemy gunners had a more difficult time tracking the Surprise Package than the standard AC-130As at night by either optical or aural tracking means.

d. Although the maximum self-destruct slant range of the 23mm AAA round is rated between 9,200 feet and 11,500 feet AGL (depending on temperature), the Surprise Package crew never experienced 23mm rounds exploding at their flight altitudes. On the other hand, the standard AC-130As operated at an altitude where they were hit by 23mm AAA. The 23mm AAA did not appear to be a serious threat to the Surprise Package aircraft.

The strike results for Surprise Package, when compared with comparable statistics on the AC-130A aircraft, proved conclusively that the test bed aircraft, despite some equipment difficulties, was the most effective individual aircraft in destroying or damaging trucks (7.34 trucks destroyed or damaged per sortie). As was expected, the standard AC-130A gunships were the next most effective truck killers in the 7AF inventory (4.34 trucks destroyed or damaged per sortie). [144]

Three subsystems deserve close attention, for they greatly enhanced the effectiveness of the weapon system. The 40mm guns were highly effective and reliable. They permitted a stand-off range of 2.0 nautical miles while still effectively destroying the target. The explosive power and accuracy of the Surprise Package 40mm guns were put to good use at Dak Seang where friendly forces were surrounded by Viet Cong forces who, in turn, were well-protected in gullies and bunkers which were situated very close to the camp. Artillery and tactical bombing were impractical. Reports received from the commander of the camp indicated that the 40mm rounds were extremely effective in blasting apart the enemy bunkers. On this close support mission, the Surprise Package flew at 5,500 feet AGL and below. Towards the end of the evaluation period, it became difficult to obtain parts for the Bofors guns, suggesting the possibility that AFSC and AFLC would have to select a more supportable 40mm gun system for the limited Surprise Package update program approved for all AC-130As.

The performance of the BLACK CROW sensor improved steadily during the evaluation. It consistently found and tracked trucks and radar through heavy haze, clouds, rain, and jungle canopy, conditions which precluded the use of the NOD, FLIR, and LLLTV. Dependent upon the skill of the operator, and during the last half of the evaluation period, this sensor initially acquired 70 percent to 80 percent of all targets detected by the Surprise Package and successfully brought the aircraft into the firing orbit to assist the NOD, FLIR, and LLLTV sensor operators in acquisition. 145/ Truck targets were routinely detected by the BLACK CROW at slant ranges in excess of six miles which significantly decreased search time. The pointing accuracy of the BLACK CROW antenna was reported to be 0.5 degrees in azimuth and elevation; however, its total system accuracy (when used as a gun laying sensor) was estimated to be approximately six milliradians. This indicates that if the BLACK CROW was to be used to fire the guns, it should be used with the 20mm guns (eight to 10 milliradian dispersion) rather than with the

40mm guns (one milliradian dispersion). The BLACK CROW was used as
the gun firing sensor on several occasions during weather; however,
no strike results were recorded. When trucks were detected by the
BLACK CROW and when the weather conditions permitted passing the target
to another sensor, the crews preferred to use the FLIR or the LLLTV
since the video tape recorder connected to each provided positive
proof of strike results. When the weather did not permit passing the
target to another sensor and the BLACK CROW had to be used for firing,
the crews reported that the target signature disappeared on the BLACK
CROW scope.

The Low Light Level TV on the Surprise Package aircraft was
mounted on a stabilized aeroflex platform installed in the crew entrance
door on the left side of the aircraft just aft of the crew compartment.
It was used to view discrete objects and terrain under light conditions
varying from bright sunlight to the low light levels encountered at
night. Its primary function was to detect and track selected targets.
On the Surprise Package aircraft two TV cameras were used: one with a
wide field of view for area search and aircraft orientation and one with
a narrow field for precise target tracking. The system was composed of
a camera, camera electronics and ancillary electronics, operator control
panel, TV monitor and camera control unit power supply. The LLLTV camera
consisted of the optics, an intensifier and a secondary electron con-
duction (SEC) vidicon tube. A remotely controlled, manually switched,
four-position iris, working in conjunction with an optical filter,

extended the range of input light levels at which the camera operated. 146/

The Surprise Package aircraft LLLTV camera tube was protected from accidental burn-out due to inadvertent exposure to high light levels such as bomb explosions, flares or fires on the ground. The protection against high light levels was provided by a micro channel plate design. The LLLTV eventually proved itself to be capable of detecting large trucks on the trails at night at slant ranges up to four nautical miles. The LLLTV became one of the primary gun laying sensors when the light level conditions permitted such action. While the illuminator was operational, it provided acceptable photo augmentation for the LLLTV. When used with the video/audio tape recorder subsystem, the LLLTV produced sufficient resolution, clarity and definition to provide excellent target imagery. The LLLTV and the video tape recorder were used successfully by both the Surprise Package and 8TFW fighter bomber aircraft to produce intelligence information for subsequent strikes. The initial problems encountered with LLLTV tube performance (primarily insufficient tube life) and LLLTV tracking (due to the sluggish or erratic platform operation) appeared to have been solved by the end of the evaluation period.

Certain deficiencies became apparent during the initial combat evaluation of Surprise Package. 147/ The most significant deficiencies were related to the proper integration of all of the individual subsystems and the maintenance of these same subsystems. The deficiency areas were identified as follows:

a. Total system integration was seldom experienced
    due to the aircraft electrical power problems and
    periods when certain subsystems were inoperative;
    however, there was usually sufficient equipment
    redundancy and/or TAC/AFSC technical and opera-
    tional expertise on-board at all times to provide
    corrective actions. Therefore, the combat effec-
    tiveness of the entire weapon system was seldom
    degraded. The aircraft and crew managed to obtain
    some of their best strike results on flights when
    there was loss of certain fire control system
    computer options.

b. Adequate and up-to-date aircraft electrical wiring
    drawings did not exist for the majority of the
    Surprise Package aircraft modifications. The lack
    of these drawings led to costly mistakes, and also
    increased the amount of time it took to perform
    subsystem failure analysis and to make the neces-
    sary repairs.

c. The aircraft experienced electrical problems which
    were associated with power transients and erratic
    sine waves from the electrical power produced by the
    AC generators. The problem manifested itself in
    several different ways: (1) generation of false
    sensor input angles which, in turn, caused "aim/
    wander" problems in the pilot's optical sight and
    large misses; (2) periodic erasures of the memory
    cores of the various computers; (3) erratic storage
    of the target coordinates in the inertial/targeting
    subsystems, and (4) erratic computations. This
    problem also affected the general performance of
    all subsystems in which the phase of the electrical
    power was critical to satisfactory operation (e.g.,
    all excitation voltages; resolver chains; the AN/
    ARN-92; 2-axis gyro; and the LTN-51). The problem
    was reduced considerably when these power critical
    subsystems were completely isolated from the AC
    generators and these same subsystems derived their
    power from a separate inverter. This electrical
    power problem was found to be common to all of the
    AC-130As.

d. The Kearfott and Aeroflex platforms initially used
    as slaved pointing devices for the 2KW illuminator
    and the LLLTV were marginal in performance. The
    direct drive torquers used in these platforms to
    compensate for roll, pitch, yaw, and G-loads were

79

inadequate for the precise slaving required. An improved platform, reworked by an Air Force Academy laboratory and containing a heavier 10 pound torquer, was shipped to Ubon during the latter portion of the evaluation period. The new platform was a considerable improvement over previous models and permitted the LLLTV operator to have smooth, accurate, and responsive tracking.

e. The 2KW illuminator was inoperative during the last three months of the period, creating the necessity to reinstall the 40KW illuminator. The 2KW illuminator lamps burned out very quickly after installation. Since the unit was never repaired, the precise nature of the deficiency remained unknown.

f. The helmet sight remained inoperative for the entire evaluation period. Maintenance manuals and qualified maintenance personnel were not available to accomplish the necessary repairs.

g. Structural problems were encountered since the first firing of the 40mm guns. Blast and projectile shock wave damaged the wing flap area. Gun recoil loosened locking bolts and the aircraft cargo floor. A new floor support was constructed in-theater that effectively eliminated the gun mount/floor flexing interaction. A team from the U.S. Air Force Academy instrumented the aircraft to measure the effects of 40mm gun recoil on the basic structure and gun mounts. The extent of this problem remains unknown and is currently under investigation.

Despite these difficulties, Surprise Package "produced results" exceeding original expectations.[148/] Surprse Package continued to fly combat missions after the initial test and evaluation period, and the aircraft continued its superlative performance.[149/] Surprise Package aircraft #54-0490 was to retain its unique configuration which allowed for continued development of specialized tactics, techniques and equipment tests, and was expected to continue setting the pace for gunship operations.[150/]

FOOTNOTES

FOREWORD

1. (S) CHECO Report, First Test and Combat Use of the FC-47, Hq PACAF, 8 December 1965;

   (S) CHECO Report, The Defense of Attopeu, Hq PACAF, 16 May 1966;

   (S) CHECO Report, The Defense of Lima Site 36, Hq PACAF, 25 May 1966; and

   (S) CHECO Report, AC-47 Operations, Hq PACAF, 14 July 1966.

2. (S) CHECO Report, Night Close Air Support in RVN, 1961-1966, Hq PACAF, 15 March 1967.

3. (S) CHECO Report, The Role of USAF Gunships in Southeast Asia, Hq PACAF, 30 August 1969.

CHAPTER I

4. (S) CHECO Report 20-104 First Test and Combat Use of the FC-47, Hq PACAF, 22 July 1965, pp. 2-3.

5. (S) Msg PACAF to 2AD, D050050 (AFEO), 15 January 1965.

6. (S) History of the 14th Air Commando Wing, 1 July - 30 September 1966, p. 47. Archives Branch, USAF Historical Division, Maxwell Air Force Base, Alabama.

7. (S) CHECO Report 20-212 The Role of USAF Gunships in Southeast Asia, Hq PACAF, 30 August 1969, p. 13.

8. (S) Ibid.

9. (S) CHECO Report 20-166 AC-47 Operations, Hq PACAF 14 July 1966, p. 7-11.

10. (S) CHECO Report, Role of USAF Gunships, 30 August 1969, p. 23.

11. (S) Ibid, pp. 17-19.

12. (S) Report, subj: End of Tour Report, 30 October 1969, by Colonel H. Heiberg, Chief AFAT-1.

13. (S) Interview, topic: VNAF AC-47 Combat Operations. With Major Nyles Courtney, USAF, Air Force Advisory Group, AFGP, DOS/C, by Captain James L. Cole, Jr., at Tan Son Nhut AB, RVN, 5 June 1971.

14. (S) CHECO Report, <u>VNAF Improvement and Modernization Program</u>, Hq PACAF, 5 February 1970, p. 80.

15. (S) <u>Ibid</u>, p. 80.

16. (U) Interview, topic: VNAF AC-47 Combat Operations. With Major Huynh Van Tong, Commander 817th CS, VNAF, by Captain James L. Cole, Jr., at Tan Son Nhut AB, RVN, 3 July 1971.

17. (S) Hq 7AF SO G-431, 27 January 1970.

18. (U) Interview, topic: VNAF AC-47 Combat Operations. With Major Pham Hiep, Chief Pilot, AC-47 Stan/Eval, VNAF, by Captain James L. Cole, Jr., at Tan Son Nhut AB, RVN, 5 June 1971.

19. (S) CHECO Report, <u>VNAF I&M Program</u>, 5 February 1970, p. 79.

20. (S) <u>Ibid</u>, p. 82.

21. (U) Interview, Major Pham Hiep, 5 June 1971.

22. (S) 432 Tactical Reconnaissance Wing History, October-December 1969, Volume I, p. 27.

23. (S) <u>Ibid</u>, p. 31.

24. (S) Extracted from 432TRW History, October-December 1969, Volume I, p. 27. Also included in the AC-47 BDA were two trucks and one 23mm gun destroyed and four 14.5mm guns silenced.

25. (S) <u>Ibid</u>, p. 28.

26. (S) 432TRW History, April-June 1970, Volume I, p. 12.

27. (S) <u>Ibid</u>, p. 25.

28. (S) Memo for the Record, Major Charles Loucks to Col. R. F. Tyrrell, AIRA, VYN, 30 August 1969.

29. (S) Ltr, AOC Savannakhet to AIRA Vientiane, subj: AOC Commander's Report, 5-11 September 1969.

30. (S) Msg, American Ambassador, Vientiane to DEPCHJUSMAGTHAI, subj: AC-47 Operations, 101102Z Dec 69.

31. (S) Interview, topic: AC-47 Combat Operations. With Lt Col D. R. Waddell, Commander, Det 1, 56th Special Operations Wing, by Captain James L. Cole, Jr., at Udorn AB, Thailand, 24 June 1971.

32. (S) Msg, JANAF Attaches to DIA, et al, subj: Joint Operational Summary, Laos, 4 February - 31 March 1971.

33. (S) The MXU-470/A gun module can be fired at either fast rate (6000 rounds per minute per gun) or slow rate (3000 rounds per minute per gun).

34. (S) Interview, topic: RLAF AC-47 Combat Operations. With Captain Anthony Hotsko, USAF Advisor to RLAF, by Lt Col Harry D. Blout at Udorn AB, Thailand, 1 April 1971.

35. (S) Msg, 7/13AF to 7AF, subj: RLAF AC-47 Capability, 270815Z Feb 1970.

36. (S) Interview, Captain Hotsko, 1 April 1971.

37. (S) Ibid.

CHAPTER II

38. (S) CHECO Report, The Role of USAF Gunships in Southeast Asia, Hq PACAF, 30 August 1969, p. 21.

39. (S) Interview, topic: Gunship Combat Operations. With Major James W. Calvert, Gunship Branch, DOPS, Hq 7AF, by Capt Cole at Tan Son Nhut AB, RVN, 10 June 1971.

40. (S) Interview, topic: AC-119G Combat Operations. With 1st Lieutenant Richard C. Marr, AC-119G Gunship pilot, 17 AB, RVN, 27 June 1971.

41. (S) Commando Hunt V, May 1971, p. 113; and

    (S) Hq PACAF XPR Ltr, subj: Project CHECO SEA Rprt: Fixed Wing Gunships in SEA, 13 Jan 72. (Hereafter cited as Hq PACAF XPR letter.)

42. (S) Ibid, p. 113.

43. (S) <u>Ibid</u>, p. 113.

44. (S) <u>Ibid</u>, p. 114.

45. (S) <u>Ibid</u>, p. 114.

46. (S) Interview, topic: AC-119G Convoy Escort Operations. With Lt Col James W. James, C Flight Commander, 17th SOS, Tan Son Nhut AB, RVN, 5 July 1971.

47. (S) <u>Ibid</u>.

48. (S) 14th Special Operations Wing History, 1 July-30 December 1970, Appendices 8 and 10, and 14th SOW History, 1 January - 31 March, Appendix 6; and

    (S) Hq PACAF XPR letter.

49. (U) 7.62mm Armor Piercing Incendiary (API) Ammunition Test Folder, Mission Reports, C Flight, 17th SOS Tan Son Nhut AB, RVN.

50. (S) <u>VNAF Plan 7052</u>, VNAF/7AF/AFGP, I&M AC-119G Activation Plan, AFGP, Tan Son Nhut AB, RVN, p. 2.

51. (S) <u>Ibid</u>, p. 3.

52. (S) Joint Program Action Directive 71-107, 30 November 1970, Appendix 1, AFGP, Tan Son Nhut AB, RVN.

53. (U) Interview, topic: VNAF AC-119G Operations. With Capt Chu-Manh Bich, AC-119G Aircraft Commander, 819th CS, by Capt Cole at Tan Son Nhut AB, RVN, 1 July 1971.

54. (U) <u>Ibid</u>.

55. (U) Interview, topic: VNAF AC-119G Operations. With Capt Gary Walker, USAF, AC-119G Instructor Pilot, 17th SOS, by Capt Cole at Tan Son Nhut AB, RVN, 26 June 1971.

56. (U) <u>Ibid</u>.

57. (U) Interview, topic: VNAF AC-119G Operations. With Major Edward Uhrich, Gunships Officer, Ops/Plans, Air Force Advisory Group (AFGP), by Capt Cole, 2 July 1971.

58. (S) 14th Special Operations Wing History, 1 January - 31 March
          1971, Appendix 9.

59. (U) Interview, Major Edward Uhrich, 2 July 1971.

60. (S) Interview, topic: AC-119K Combat Operations. With Major
          James Calvert, 10 June 1971;

    (S) Hq PACAF DOOF Ltr, subj: Project CHECO Report, Fixed Wing Gun-
          ships in SEA, 11 Jan 72; and

    (S) Hq PACAF XPR letter.

61. (S) Ibid.

62. (S) Interview, topic: AC-119K Combat Operations. With Major
          Burt Wallin, Chief of Gunships Branch, DOPS, Hq 7AF, by
          Mr. Mel Porter at Tan Son Nhut AB, RVN, 11 April 1971.

63. (S) Ibid.

64. (S) 14th Special Operations Wing History, 1 July-30 September
          1970, Appendix 9 and 1 October-31 December 1970 Appendix 10; and

    (S) Hq PACAF XPR letter.

65. (S) Ibid.

66. (S) Ibid.

67. (S) Interview, Major Burt Wallin, 11 April 1971.

68. (S) Ibid.

69. (S) 14th Special Operations Wing History, 1 January-31 March
          1971, p. 10.

70. (S) Ibid, p. 9.

71. (S) Ltr, Samuel J. Scott, Acting Director of Operations Analysis,
          to General Petit, located in 14th SOW History, 1 January-31 March
          1971, Appendix 6.

72. (S) Commando Hunt V, May 1971, p. 263.

CHAPTER III

73. (S) CHECO Report, <u>The Role of USAF Gunships in Southeast Asia</u>, Hq PACAF, 30 August 1969, p. 25.

74. (S) Msg, General Ryan to General McConnel, subj: Gunship II Requirements, 12 February 1969.

75. (S) Evaluation period lasted from 27 February 1968 to 14 May 1969. CHECO Report, <u>Role of USAF Gunships in SEA</u>, p. 27.

76. (S) Ltr, Capt H. W. Welch, Unit Historian, Det 2, 14 SOW, 1 March 1969, p. 5.

77. (S) CHECO Report, <u>Role of USAF Gunships in SEA</u>, p. 28.

78. (S) Working Paper, 16th SOS, subj: An AFSC View of Spectre Tactics, undated.

79. (S) CHECO Report, Role of USAF Gunships in SEA, provides a detailed explanation of the gunship/escort tactic on page 30 and pages 40 through 43.

80. (S) Specific technical descriptions of particular subsystems were extracted from Commando Hunt III, May 1970, DOA 70-300, Appendix C.

81. (S) Interview, topic: AC-130 Operations. With Major Eugene L. Alsperger former IR Operator, 16th SOS, Ubon RTAFB, by Captain Drue DeBerry at Tan Son Nhut Air Base, RVN, 28 August 1971.

82. (S) 16th Special Operations Squadron History, July-September 1970, Appendix F.

83. (S) Commando Hunt III, May 1970, DOA 70-300, Appendix C, p. 185.

84. (S) <u>Ibid</u>, p. 87.

85. (S) <u>Commando Hunt V</u>, May 1971, Hq 7AF, p. 253.

86. (S) Commando Hunt V was the concentrated air campaign designed to interdict the overland flow of supplies through Laos to the Viet Cong and North Vietnamese forces in South Vietnam. This campaign spanned the 1970-71 dry season in Laos and covered the period 10 October 1970 through 30 April 1971.

87. (S) Msg, 7AF to 8TFW, subj: AC-130 Performance, 291130Z Apr 70.

88. (S) Msg, General Momyer to General Meyer, subject: Increase Gunship Fleet, 210009Z Jan 70.

89. (U) TACM 55-249, Aircrew Operational Procedures, AC-119 and AC-130, 30 Jan 70, DAF, TAC, Langley AFB, Va., p. 2-1.

90. (S) Hq PACAF DOOFS Review, 20 Jan 72.

91. (S) Ltr, DCO 8TFW to 7AF (DOCO), 22 Jun 69.

92. (S) 16th Special Operations Squadron History, April - June 1970, p. 4.

93. (S) 16th Special Operations Squadron History, January - March 1971, p. 19.

94. (S) Ibid, Annex B.

95. (S) 16th Special Operations Squadron History, January - March 1970, p. 19.

96. (S) Ibid, p. 24.

97. (S) 16th Special Operations Squadron History, April - June 1970, p. 28.

98. (S) Ltr, SOFLO to SAWC, subj: SOFLO Activity Report 3-71, 1 May 1971.

99. (S) 16th Special Operations Squadron History, January - March 1971, p. 18.

100. (S) Ibid, p. 4.

101. (S) Ibid, p. 20.

102. (S) 16th Special Operations Squadron Classified PIF/CIF, PAVE MACE Folder.

103. (S) Interview, topic: Black Crow. With Captain Richard Malchok, S/E Navigator, 16th Special Operations Squadron, by Capt Cole at Ubon RTAFB, Thailand, 17 June 1971.

104. (S) 16th Special Operations Squadron Classified PIF/CIF, PAVE MACE Folder.

105. (S) Ibid.

106. (S) Mission report contained in Ibid.

107. (S) Ibid.

108. (S) Msg, 8TFW to 7AF/DOP/DOA, subj: Misch Metal 40mm Ammunition, Attachment DD, 16th SOS History, January - March 1971.

109. (S) Ibid.

110. (S) Ibid.

111. (S) Interview, topic: AC-130 BDA, with Captain Randy Vincent, AC-130 Pilot, 16th SOS, by Capt Cole, 18 June 1971.

112. (S) Commando Hunt V, May 1971, Hq 7AF, p. 66; and

     (S) Hq PACAF DOOF Ltr, subj: Project CHECO Report, Fixed Wing Gunships in SEA, 11 Jan 72.

113. (S) CHECO Report Lam Son 719, Hq PACAF, p. 128.

114. (S) Ibid, Figure 16, p. 128.

115. (S) Secret Working Paper, subj: Gunship Operations Against Armor During Lam Son 719, DOA, Hq 7AF.

116. (S) Ibid.

117. (S) Ibid.

118. (S) Interview, topic: AC-130 Close Air Support for TIC During Lam Son 719, with Lt Col James Kyle, AC-130 Aircraft Commander and Gunship Officer, DOPS, Hq 7AF, by Capt Cole, 17 June 1971.

119. (S) Rprt, subj: Lam Son 719 After Action Report, 30 January - 6 April 1971, by Hq XXIV Corps, Dept of the Army, p. 1-F-5.

120. (S) Msg, subj: TACLO Activity Report 10-71, 25 April - 8 May 1971, p. 6.

121. (S) 16th Special Operations Squadron History, January - March 1971, Attachment CC.

122. (S) Ibid.

123. (S) Msg, subj: TACLO Activity Report 10-71, 25 Apr-8 May 1971, p. 5.

124. (S) Ibid, p. 6.

125. (S) Rprt, subj: Evaluation of AC-130 Gunship Munitions, 30 May 1971, by DOP, Hq 7AF.

126. (S) Msg, subj: TACLO Activity Report 11-71, 9 May-22 May 1971, p. 5.

127. (S) For a complete listing of Evaluation's conclusions see Appendix K.

128. (S) Msg, General Abrams to Admiral McCain, subj: AC-130 BDA Criteria, 310140Z May 1971.

129. (S) Ibid.

130. (S) Interview, topic: AC-130 BDA, with Captain Randy Vincent, AC-130 Pilot, 16th SOS, by Capt Cole, 18 June 1971. For additional information from ASD regarding the effectiveness of 40mm ammunition, see Appendix J.

131. (S) Rprt, subj: Minutes of PAVE SPECTRE Gunship Conference, 30 March-2 April 1971, Wright-Patterson AFB, Ohio, p. 1-3. See Appendix L for a listing of PAVE SPECTRE subsystems configuration.

132. (S) Ibid, p. 1-3.

133. (S) <u>Commando Hunt III</u>, May 1970, DOA 70-300, p. xvii.

134. (S) <u>Commando Hunt V</u>, May 1971, Hq 7AF, p. 61.

CHAPTER IV

135. (S) History, 16th Special Operations Squadron June-September 1970, Appendix A (Combat Evaluation: Surprise Package Aircraft, Hq 7AF June 1970.)

136. (S) <u>Ibid</u>.

137. (S) <u>Ibid</u>.

138. (S) <u>Ibid</u>.

139. (S) <u>Ibid</u>.

140. (S) <u>Commando Hunt III</u>, May 1970, DOA 70-300, p. 186.

141. (S) <u>Ibid</u>, p. 183.

142. (S) <u>Commando Hunt III</u>, May 1970, DOA 70-300, p. 182.

143. (S) Extract, History, 16th Special Operations Squadron, June-September 1970, Appendix A.

144. (S) Report, subj: "Commando Hunt III," May 1970, DOA 70-300.

145. (S) History, 16th Special Operations Squadron June-September 1970, Appendix A.

146. (S) <u>Ibid</u>,

147. (S) Extract, History, 16th Special Operations Squadron, June-September 1970, Appendix A.

148. (S) History, 16th Special Operations Squadron, January-March 1970, p. 29.

149. (S) History, 16th Special Operations Squadron, April-June 1970, p. 30.

150. (S) Minutes, PAVE SPECTRE Gunship Conference, 30 March-2 April 1971, p. 1-3.

APPENDIX A

USAF LATERAL FIRING GUNSHIP MISSION EFFECTIVENESS

	LOCAL BASE DEFENSE	HAMLET DEFENSE	ARMY SUPPORT	DAY/NIGHT ALL WEATHER INTERDICT	ARMED RECONNAISSANCE AND HARASSMENT	HUNTER/ KILLER
AC-130	* * * *	* * * *	* * * *	* *	* * * *	* * * *
AC-119K	* * *	* * * *	* * *	* *	* * * *	* * *
AC-119G	* *	*	*		* *	*
AC-47	* *	*	*		*	*

Qualitative Value Judgment: Based on Firepower, Aircraft Capability, Sensors

APPENDIX B

SUMMARY OF GUNSHIP SORTIES BY AIRCRAFT TYPE AND MISSION

		Strike	Armed Recon	CAS	Air Int	Total Attk	Recon	Rescap	Tng	Maint	Other	Tot Cmbt Support
1JAN-30JUN70	AC-130	38	764	4	4	810	2	0	0	0	2	4
	AC-119	147	739	1452	156	2494	0	2	49	132	832	1197
	AC-47	273	3	1190	0	1466	3	0	459	43	668	1402
1JUL-31DEC70	AC-130	149	147	1	18	315	72	0	7	1	7	89
	AC-119	127	398	553	972	2030	8	1	112	167	720	1213
	AC-47	0	0	826	1	827	0	3	394	46	1780	2449
1JAN-31MAR71	AC-130	0	893	16	3	912	115	0	3	1	1	120
	AC-119	10	731	160	583	1414	3	1	79	82	247	465
	AC-47	0	0	240	0	240	0	0	164	16	994	1300
1APR-15JUN71	AC-130	0	652	17	13	682	9	0	6	17	6	49
	AC-119	12	657	112	474	1255	0	0	132	77	212	452
	AC-47	0	0	173	2	175	0	0	137	26	712	990

GUNSHIP ATTACK PATTERN

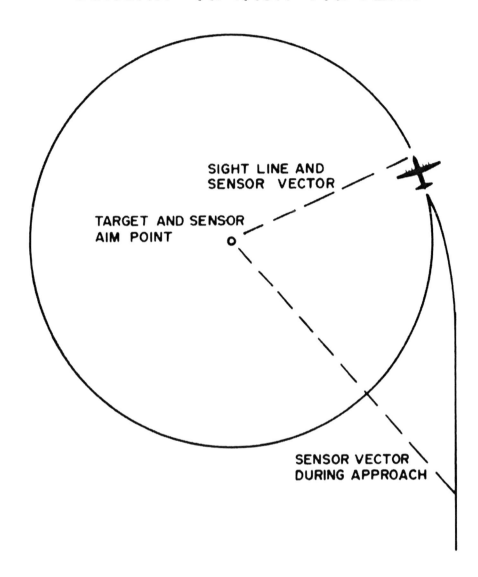

SIGHT LINE AND
SENSOR VECTOR

TARGET AND SENSOR
AIM POINT

SENSOR VECTOR
DURING APPROACH

BASIC FIRING GEOMETRY (NO WIND – NO OFFSET)

GUNSHIP ATTACK PATTERN

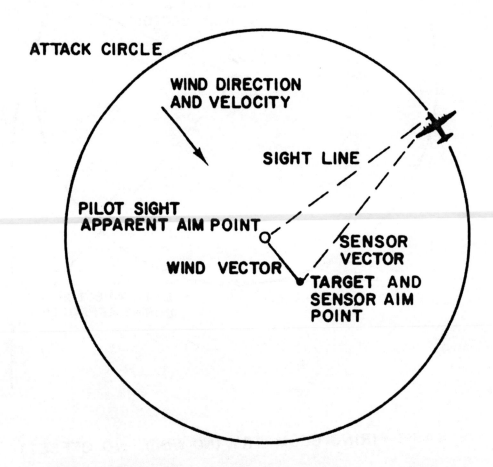

ATTACK CIRCLE

WIND DIRECTION
AND VELOCITY

SIGHT LINE

PILOT SIGHT
APPARENT AIM POINT

SENSOR
VECTOR

WIND VECTOR

TARGET AND
SENSOR AIM
POINT

FIRING GEOMETRY (WIND CORRECTED—NO OFFSET)

GUNSHIP ATTACK PATTERN

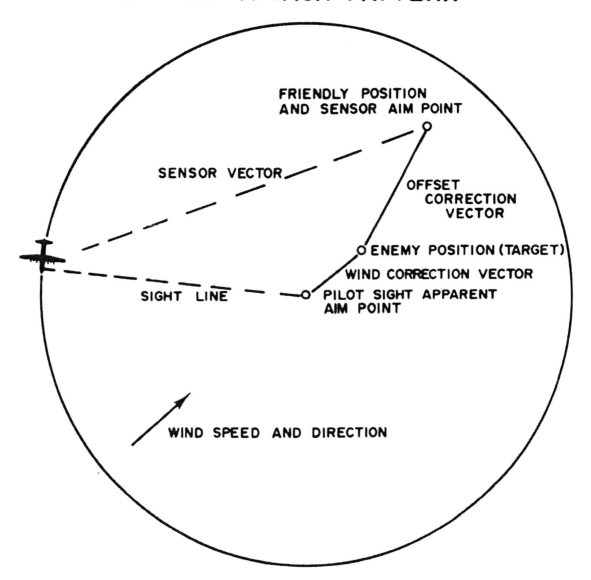

FRIENDLY POSITION
AND SENSOR AIM POINT

SENSOR VECTOR

OFFSET
CORRECTION
VECTOR

ENEMY POSITION (TARGET)

WIND CORRECTION VECTOR

SIGHT LINE

PILOT SIGHT APPARENT
AIM POINT

WIND SPEED AND DIRECTION

FIRING GEOMETRY (OFFSET AND WIND CORRECTED)

APPENDIX F

AC-119G BATTLE DAMAGE SUMMARY: 1 JAN 70 - 30 MAY 71

Date	Aircraft Tail Number	Damaged or Lost	Enemy Weapon
12 JAN 70	069	D	SA
13 MAY 70	170	D	12.7mm
25 JUL 70	192	D	SA
20 Aug 70	069	D	Unknown
6 DEC 70	136	D	12.7mm
25 JAN 71	851	D	SA
19 MAY 71	115	D	SA

SOURCE: Combat D & D Listing, DOA, Hq 7th AF

APPENDIX G

AC-119K BATTLE DAMAGE SUMMARY: 1 JAN 70 - 30 MAY 71

Date	Aircraft Tail Number	Damaged or Lost	Enemy Weapon
5 FEB 70	826	D	23mm
1 MAR 70	830	D	23mm
23 APR 70	154	D	SA
23 APR 70	935	D	23mm
27 APR 70	879	D	37mm
8 MAY 70	883	D	37mm
27 AUG 70	826	D	12.7mm
4 JAN 71	826	D	23mm
16 JAN 71	982	D	23mm
11 FEB 71	854	D	Unknown
29 MAR 71	148	D	Unknown
15 MAY 71	850	D	23mm

SOURCE: Combat D & D Listing, DOA, Hq 7th AF

APPENDIX H

AC-130 BATTLE DAMAGE SUMMARY: 1 JAN 70 - 30 MAY 71

Date	Aircraft Tail Number	Damaged or Lost	Enemy Weapon
19 FEB 70	628	D	37mm
19 FEB 70	129	D	37mm
21 MAR 70	628	D	37mm
27 MAR 70	490	D	37mm
8 APR 70	490	D	SA
16 APR 70	129	D	37mm
22 APR 70	625	L	37mm
5 MAY 70	623	D	37mm
6 MAY 70	129	D	37mm
21 NOV 70	129	D	37mm
12 DEC 70	509	D	37mm
6 JAN 71	029	D	37mm
21 JAN 71	044	D	37mm
21 JAN 71	040	D	37mm
22 JAN 71	469	D	37mm
23 JAN 71	044	D	37mm
26 JAN 71	623	D	37mm
29 JAN 71	469	D	37mm
10 FEB 71	490	D	57mm
18 FEB 71	509	D	37mm

Date	Aircraft Tail Number	Damaged or Lost	Enemy Weapon
25 MAR 71	129	D	57mm
30 MAR 71	046	D	Unknown
2 APR 71	509	D	Unknown
8 APR 71	630	D	37mm
9 APR 71	014	D	37mm
13 APR 71	509	D	37mm
14 APR 71	628	D	37mm
15 APR 71	014	D	Unknown
15 APR 71	469	D	37mm
18 APR 71	029	D	37mm
20 APR 71	043	D	37mm
24 APR 71	469	D	37mm
3 MAY 71	490	D	37mm
9 MAY 71	046	D	37mm

SOURCE: Combat D & D Listing, DOA, Hq 7th AF

APPENDIX I

AC-130 STANDARD ORDNANCE LOADS

"DRY SEASON":

    40mm Ammunition: 640 Rounds (40 cans)

    20mm Ammunition: 3,000 Rounds

    Mk 6: 15 with flare launcher
          20 without flare launcher

    Mk 24: 24 installed with flare launcher

"WET SEASON":

    40mm Ammunition: 448 Rounds (28 cans)

    20mm Ammunition: 3,000 Rounds plus 17 cans
          secured in aisle

    Mk 6: 15 with flare launcher
          20 without flare launcher

    Mk 24: 24 installed with flare launcher

SOURCE: 16th SOS PIF #47-71

APPENDIX J

Information on 40mm Effectiveness from ASD
(Aeronautical Systems Division, AFSC, USAF)

HIT DESCRIPTION	W/O SECONDARIES	WITH SECONDARIES
Beyond 10 Feet	No Damage	Destroyed
Short Inside 10 Feet	Possible Damage	Destroyed
Long Inside 10 Feet	No Damage	Destroyed
Right or Left Inside 10 Feet	Possible Damage	Destroyed
Direct Hit on Cab or Bed	Damaged	Destroyed
Direct Hit on Hood	Damaged	Destroyed

CRITERIA:

    Possible Damage - 50% Require over 1 Hour to Repair

        Damaged   - 90% Require over 1 Hour to Repair

        Destroyed   - Burning or Exploding Truck

SOURCE: ASD MSG 05 2104Z MAR 71
            SUBJ: 40mm FIRING TESTS RESULTS

APPENDIX K

12 MAY 1971 EVALUATION OF GUNSHIP MUNITIONS

Prepared by Directorate of Operations Plans,
Headquarters 7th Air Force, 30 May 1971

CONCLUSIONS:

1. A sustained fire will destroy a truck.

2. Near misses by 20mm or 40mm projectiles cause little or
   no damage to a truck.

3. Fuel tanks seldom receive direct hits, and diesel fuel in
   the tanks does not ignite even on a burning truck.

4. Fragments from either 20mm or 40mm projectiles impacting
   on or near a truck can puncture tires.

5. The 40mm Misch Metal projectiles do not have any greater
   effect on an empty truck than standard HEI.

6. Test results substantiate the parts of the revised truck
   kill criteria for gunships which state that a sustained
   fire destroys a truck and a direct hit without secondary
   explosion or sustained damages a truck.

7. Present procedures used by the AC-130 gunship to determine
   target coordinates for RF-4C aircraft night photography
   appear accurate enough to insure that the target falls
   within the camera coverage.

APPENDIX L

PAVE SPECTRE SUBSYSTEMS CONFIGURATION

SENSORS:

LLLTV*
GMTI Processor (APN-59 Radar)*
IR Set (AAD-7)*
BLACK CROW*
APQ-150*

FIRE CONTROL SYSTEM:

Digital Fire Control Computer
IMU
Heads Up Display (Gunsight)
Fire Control Display
SSIU
Boresight Box*
Fire Control Teleprinter
Moving Map Display
Air Data System
Sensor Slaving Unit (MSU)*
2 Gyro Platform*

Other:

Helmet Sight*
Laser Ranger Designator
2 KW Illuminator*
BDA Airborne Recorder*
APR-36/37
Trim-7A*
Survivability Package
40mm (2)*
20mm (2)*
7.62mm (2)*
AIC-18/25*
SLADS*
LAU-74 Flare Launcher*
ARN-92

* Items common to PAVE PRONTO

SOURCE: Minutes of PAVE SPECTRE GUNSHIP CONFERENCE,
         30 March - 2 April 1971

APPENDIX M

Altitude: A - 2,500' AGL

B - 3,500' AGL

C - 4,500' AGL

D - 5,500' AGL

E - 6,500' AGL

F - 7,500' AGL

G - 8,500' AGL

H - 9,500' AGL (Standard Firing Altitude)

SOURCE: Hq PACAF (DOOFS) Review, 20 Jan 72

GLOSSARY

AAA	Antiaircraft Artillery
ABCCC	Airborne Battlefield Command and Control
AC	Aircraft Commander
AFGP	Air Force Advisory Group
AFSC	Air Force Systems Command
AGL	Above Ground Level
AIRA	Air Attache
AM	Amplitude Modulation
ARRS	Aerospace Rescue and Recovery Squadron
ARVN	Army of the Republic of Vietnam
ASAP	As Soon As Possible
ASD	Aerospace Systems Division
AW	Automatic Weapon
BC	Black Crow
BDA	Battle Damage Assessment
BR	Barrel Roll
CAP	Combat Air Patrol
CAS	Close Air Support
CINCPACAF	Commander-in-Chief, Pacific Air Forces
CL	Combat Loss
CONUS	Continental United States
CP	Copilot
CS	Combat Squadron
CSAF	Chief of Staff, United States Air Force
DASC	Direct Air Support Center
DMZ	Demilitarized Zone
FAG	Forward Air Guide
FAC	Forward Air Controller
FCF	Functional Check Flight
FLIR	Forward Looking Infrared
FLR	Forward Looking Radar
FM	Frequency Modulation
FOL	Forward Operating Location
HEI	High Explosive Incendiary
HF	High Frequency

I&M	Improvement and Modernization
IO	Information Office(r)
IP	Instructor Pilot
IR	Infrared
KBA	Killed by Air
KEL	Known Enemy Location
KM	Kilometer
KW	Kilowatt
LLLTV	Low-Light-Level Television
LOC	Line of Communication
LORAN	Long Range Airborne Navigation
LTV	Ling Temco Vought
mm	Millimeter
MR	Military Region
MSL	Mean Sea Level
MTT	Mobile Training Team
NM	Nautical Mile
NOD	Night Observation Device
NVA	North Vietnamese Army
PACAF	Pacific Air Forces
PDJ	Plaine des Jarres
PL	Pathet Lao
POL	Petroleum, Oil, and Lubricants
RHAW	Radar Homing and Warning
RLAF	Royal Laotian Air Force
RLG	Royal Laotian Government
RTB	Return to Base
RTAFB	Royal Thai Air Force Base
RVN	Republic of Vietnam
RVNAF	Republic of Vietnam Armed Forces
SA	Small Arms
SEA	Southeast Asia
SEADAB	Southeast Asia Data Base File
SEL	Suspected Enemy Location
SOS	Special Operations Squadron
SOW	Special Operations Wing
STOL	Short Takeoff and Landing

TAC	Tactical Air Command
TACLO	Tactical Air Command Liaison Officer
TACAN	Tactical Air Navigation
TACC	Tactical Air Control Center
TAS	True Airspeed
TFW	Tactical Fighter Wing
TIC	Troops in Contact
TOT	Time over Target
UE	Unit Equipment
UHF	Ultra High Frequency
Unk	Unknown
UTM	Universal Transverse Mercator
VC	Viet Cong
VHF	Very High Frequency
VNAF	Vietnamese Air Force
WAIS	Weekly Air Intelligence Summary
ZIL	A Soviet built truck
ZPU	A Soviet built automatic weapon

PACAF - HAFB, Hawaii

Lightning Source UK Ltd.
Milton Keynes UK
UKOW020753230512

193107UK00004B/7/P